Luck

3. 2/20/11

4/9/11 - 49   7 wks

5/14/11 - 84   12 wks

6/19/11 - 112   16 wks

Revolutionary
Rapid Training
Method...Dog
Health & Care

FAMILY
DOG

by

RICHARD A.
WOLTERS

Author of HOME DOG, KID'S DOG,
GAME DOG, WATER DOG,
and GUN DOG

Introduction by
Red Smith

A DUTTON BOOK

DUTTON
Published by the Penguin Group
Penguin Books USA Inc., 375 Hudson Street, New York, New York 10014, U.S.A.
Penguin Books Ltd, 27 Wrights Lane, London W8 5TZ, England
Penguin Books Australia Ltd, Ringwood, Victoria, Australia
Penguin Books Canada Ltd, 10 Alcorn Avenue, Toronto, Ontario, Canada M4V 3B2
Penguin Books (N.Z.) Ltd, 182-190 Wairau Road, Auckland 10, New Zealand

Penguin Books Ltd, Registered Offices:
Harmondsworth, Middlesex, England

Published by Dutton, an imprint of New American Library,
a division of Penguin Books USA Inc.
Distributed in Canada by McClelland & Stewart Inc.
32   31   30   29

All photographs with the exceptions listed below are by Roger Wolters.
Endpapers and pages 68, 75, 76, 94, by Joan Sydlow
Jacket photograph by Joan Sydlow

 REGISTERED TRADEMARK—MARCA REGISTRADA

LIBRARY OF CONGRESS CATALOG CARD NUMBER: 63-8611
ISBN: 0-525-24554-5
Printed in the United Statess of America
Book and jacket design by Richard A. Wolters

Dedicated to Kids and Dogs

Contents

Introduction

It should be stated at the outset that the author of this book is some kind of a nut, or something. His taste in haberdashery is — well, perhaps the adjective is "uninhibited." He wears a mustache that reminds some thoughtful observers of Chaplin and some of Menjou and some of a way-stop in between.

He has no special enthusiasm for standard beds in conventional houses. He prefers to sleep in a vehicle which he calls a "camper" and you or I would call a bus. It is a small bus with handsomely curtained windows, the curtains cut, fitted, and stitched by a spouse whose patience, understanding, and indulgence should serve as an example to spouses everywhere. (Or spice? Plurals always give me trouble.)

Our author, to repeat, enjoys sleeping in this bus, conventionally attired in pajamas of staid cut and pattern. There is nothing whatever unusual about the pajamas, unless you count the harness and shoulder holster containing a large, lethal roscoe which he wears outside.

Our author enjoys fishing and hunting, which certainly does not mark him as unusual. What does set him apart from some zillions of fellow citizens is that when he goes fishing he casts a fly supremely well, and when he goes hunting he hits what he shoots at.

When he sets out to train a dog — and here we get to the meat of the subject — he does not go sit at the feet of some picturesque Maine guide listening to old husbands' tales about how you got to wait till this here pup is a year old, anyways, before you start tryin' to teach him anything. He goes instead to a research laboratory where scientists are engaged in learning how a dog thinks. Here he is advised that a puppy starts getting smart, and amenable to instruction, exactly seven weeks after he is whelped.

Dick Wolters goes home and tries it out. It works. This is un-American. It is disrespectful of Maine guides. But it works. Dick Wolters, with his knotheaded, newfangled notions, keeps training dogs and they keep turning out perfect gentlemen.

Then he writes books about how it's done, but he doesn't simply put down the words, like a proper author. He takes pictures, scads of pictures. Then he puts the pictures in the book, so that instead of just telling you how to train a dog he shows you, step by step, how any intelligent child can do it.

It is a well-known fact that keeping a dog can be just as much trouble as keeping a woman. Mr. Wolters undertakes to show that it can also be just as much fun. Chances are there is something subversive about this.

RED SMITH
The New York Herald Tribune

Author's Note

As I reach for the keys of the typewriter, the first sentence all figured out, the door of the study opens and in pops a head. My ideas fly to the wind. Daughter Gretchen bursts in to show a new dress to be worn tomorrow, the first day of second grade. She bubbles out as fast as she had gushed in.

Now the door is open. The next to enter is Tar, the big black Labrador retriever. He sniffs, puts his head on my work table (that's how big he is now), waits for a pat, turns, and once again I'm alone. Come to think of it, day after tomorrow he also starts second grade . . . he's going hunting for the first time. These intruders are the real heroine and hero of this book. As you thumb through, you'll see how cooperatively and enthusiastically they learned their lessons.

It was a lot of work for both of them, but the fact that my son Roger and I took over 2500 pictures for this book is enough proof. Tomorrow Roger starts tenth grade, and he starts it with a new skill. The pictures show what a fine photographer he has become. I'm not sure who should thank whom, but anyway, thanks, Rog, for a job well done.

Newton saw an apple fall from a tree and got the idea of gravity, but he was smart. I didn't get the idea for this book; a friend gave it to me. Women are so smart. Here's how she got the idea.

I was visiting an old friend, a boy I grew up with in Philadelphia. I've known his wife almost as long as I've known him. I had the manuscript of the first book of this series, *Gun Dog*, with me and I was explaining my new theories of dog training to Dr. Donald Jay Ottenberg and his wife Martha. As I recall it, it was either getting late or my enthusiastic, exuberant expounding of the theory of early dog training caused Martha to respond by going to sleep on the living room couch. After what seemed to me like an interesting short monologue, Martha woke up in an hour or so, sat up, stretched, blinked, and mumbled something about she was sorry she was so sleepy but she had a tough day with the kids and Chiquita Mañana. The latter is their dog, half Chihuahua or other, mixed with something else. "Why don't you do me a favor and if you do, every mother in America will love you," she continued, rubbing her sleepy head. "After you tell the hunter how to train his dog, write a book to show the kids how to train and take the responsibility of the family's best friend. It's the kid's dog, yet I have all the work." She went back to sleep. Up she popped again, wide-eyed. "Can your training method be used on the kids?"

The apple fell from the tree. I liked the idea, especially the part about every mother in the country loving me.

Martha, here's the book. Try it on Chiquita and the kids, too.

In my first book, *Gun Dog*, Gene Hill of the Jockey Hollow Field Trial Club was given credit for keeping me up late, drinking my whisky, and arguing all my dog facts point by point. He gets the same credit in this book, with an added starter. Being quite a gourmet, he became enthusiastic about my liverwurst sandwiches. I didn't mind the added expense of all the sandwiches I had to feed him to keep him on the job, but I did object to all the liverwurst smudges on the manuscript.

My thanks to Scott Bartlett, my editor at E. P. Dutton, who noted that this was the first manuscript that he had ever handled that smelled good enough to eat.

Now Tar and I have some joint thank-you's to Drs. Leo A. Wuori and Edward Grano, Jr. for checking my medical facts and theories. If man's best friend is a dog, a dog's best friend is an understanding vet.

My thanks to Dr. J. Paul Scott and his research team at the Animal Behavior Lab, Hamilon Station, of the Roscoe B. Jackson Memorial Laboratory, Mount Desert Island, Maine, for making my visit with them a most productive one. The experiments they're conducting on dogs are to help man understand himself better. But, as a by-product of this research, man can understand dog better and then dog can understand man better. Tar thanks them for this.

Tar and I agree, Dr. James A. Baker of Cornell University should receive not only our thanks, but the thanks of every dog owner. His work has helped control the most dreaded dog killer — distemper. My thanks to him for his time to explain to a mere layman the intricate details and progress of his work.

As you can see, this was a project of family and friends, and the hub of such a wheel is always the wife. Olive, thanks for letting us bring four more dirty feet into our home.

R. A. W.

2

Part I

Chapter 1

Why This Book?

Dog books have been written in English for over five hundred years. If a man is going to sit and write another one to add to the long list, he better have something new and important to say or do his barking up another tree. And so, with that firmly in mind . . .

This book is *Family Dog*. It's not about the dog's family, it's about yours. The dog's going to become a member of your family, and like the rest of the family he's going to become a good citizen. But what's new and important? Why add this book to the thousands of books that have been written? Here is a training method that's foolproof; it's a new method of training, it's revolutionary, it's fast, and most important — it's easy.

If this book had been written five hundred years ago it would've been called *A Treatyse of Dogges as Compannyones*, but this book couldn't have been written back then . . . they didn't know what we know about dogs today. As a matter of fact, this book couldn't have been written even as recently as five years ago.

The first breakthrough in understanding the psychology of what actually goes on inside the noggin of man's best friend was accomplished by scientists working at the Hamilton Station Animal Behavior Laboratory. It's important here to tell you that we're going to show you how to teach a dog in weeks what it was always thought took years to accomplish.

Stop and thumb through the pages; note the pictures. They're not photographs of a *trained* dog being put through his routine for the camera. Like no other book, we're documenting the learning process of both dog and trainer. Gretchen, our heroine, is not just re-creating a part for the pictures; she is learning in a real situation. Practically all the pictures were taken before Tar, our hero, was four months old. It's hard for people to believe that so much can be accomplished with a puppy in such a short period of time. Actually, in about twelve hours of work — that is, ten minutes a day for a couple of months — your new friend will be completely schooled and ready for his graduation.

Gun Dog, the first book in this series, was the first book to explain step by step how to train a hunting dog . . . fast. The upland bird hunter has

3

learned tnat the complicated job of training pointing dogs can be taught so that a setter or a pointer puppy can be hunting in great style by the time he's five or six months old. New training methods and techniques were used. Up until that book was written, hunting dogs weren't even started in their training until they were a year old. The outstanding success of *Gun Dog*, for the hunter, prompted this book for the family who wants a pet, not a pest.

Twenty-nine of the 30 million dogs in this country are either "doglinquent" flea bags or affectionate parasites. For nothing more than a little companionship they get free room and board, medicare, and social security. They get all this plush living plus unemployment compensation only because they have learned one trick — to wag the tail and look happy when the family comes home. Don't classify dogs as dumb animals when it's man who goes out all day to toil by the sweat of his brow in order to feed the family . . . including Towser. Meanwhile, back home in the easy chair Towser rests up so he's fresh and alert when he welcomes Master home after a rough day in the cruel world.

Why does all this take place? Some member of the family decides that Junior or Daughter should have a dog for a pet. That someone could have been Junior or Daughter themselves.

Actually, it works like this: most of the dogs in the country are bought as pets for the kids in the family. If there are a few reluctant adults who hold out against the idea of the new member of the family, there is no need here to go into a detailed account of the shenanigans by which they're cajoled into a change of heart. To explain this common phenomenon would take another book entitled something like *The American Family Structure*, and subtitled "The Kids Always Win."

But there's no real need for such a book. You've already picked up this one. The decision has been made. You're getting a dog, a new member of the family, most likely for a child. The odds are that your puppy will end up being a pest if you do what most families do. If it were a human puppy coming into the household, the whole family would be making preparations for months. But since it's a dog puppy, the kennel man is paid, a few feeding instructions are gotten, and Towser is deposited in his new home.

There's great joy and excitement . . . for the first week or so. Gradually the novelty of the new member wears off and all the burdens of feeding, housebreaking, and any other problems fall to Mother. Now in most cases, Mother has a few other things that she might have to do. She has had little or no experience in bringing up a dog, so there are two obvious alternatives.

One, Towser is put out the back door to become someone else's problem. Towser becomes a doglinquent, grows into doghood uneducated. He doesn't know good manners; he can't even write his own name let alone get a "college" education and lead a useful life. Two, Towser is kept home, but just exists around the house. In both cases it's a rather unrewarding life for dog and/or master.

Actually it doesn't take too much time or know-how to train a dog to become a good useful citizen. But it's not only the dog that has to be trained. The children of the household should be shown how to train the dog. Giving a child a dog with the understanding that it will be his or her responsibility to care for and train can be a very rewarding experience for the whole family . . . including Towser.

The book is divided into three distinct parts. First, we'll give the necessary background material: how to select the puppy and the new training philosophy based on scientific findings. We'll tell you how a dog learns and how to set up school so that he'll learn.

Part II was the real fun in producing the book. We've completely documented the development of a Labrador puppy and his trainer, six-year-old Gretchen. We have thousands of photographs from the moment they came together. We've only used those pictures that best illustrate the learning processes of both dog and child. Both were excellent students. The important thing is you'll be able to read and you'll be able to *see* how to train a dog, also how to train a child to train a dog.

Picture sequences are used extensively to *show* the child what's expected of him. You'll *see* what's expected of the dog, and where necessary, pictures will *explain* how to teach the child to teach the dog.

Part III is the general care, medical knowledge, and essential information that you should have at your fingertips. Our job here isn't to take the place of the veterinarian. These will be helpful hints that even the pediatrician wants every mother to know.

A six-year-old child can train a dog with help and guidance from an adult, so anyone six, or older, with some guidance can train a dog. The phrase "or older" may fit you better, since you may be getting a puppy as a companion for yourself. Whichever, we also said "with some guidance." This book with its "how to" pictures and background material is that guidance. Any teenager can be considered adult enough for the purposes of this book.

Sound simple? It is.

Chapter 2

Selecting the Family Dog

Dogs come in all shapes and sizes. Long-hair, short-hair, wire-hair, curly-hair, and even no-hair. Some are tall, short, toy, and tiny; they come black, brown, blond, even red, white, and blue, and all sorts of mixtures and combinations thereof.

There's a long list to choose from. The American Kennel Club recognizes 116 different breeds, some of which are a strange-looking lot. These are the purebreds and their pedigrees are probably in better order than yours or your wife's relations.

This list isn't all, not by a long shot. The membership of the more democratic "57 Variety" Club, with its astronomical numbers of unrecognized members, really swells the list for you to consider.

About the old saying, "You can pick your friends but not your relatives," we won't worry about picking your relations — we've already said that their pedigrees aren't so good. But as to your best friend, your dog, he's worth worrying about.

If you're going to have a best friend it's only fair to him and to you that you find out all about him. You're going to be living together . . . for a long time.

All puppies are cute — they all like to cuddle up, they all like to lick your face, they're all little fluffballs, but remember, some grow to weigh five pounds and some grow to be 155 or better. What are your needs in a dog? Lie down on a couch and ask yourself some questions. What kind of a dog would you look best with? What kind would fit your home? Will the dog require plenty of exercise? Will one of the long-hair varieties that shed cause the second parlormaid to look for employment elsewhere? Dog care is time-consuming. Short-hair dogs are easy to manage. What kind of climate do you live in? A long-hair suffers in heat. Will your budget stand for weekly beauty parlor appointments? A poodle is like a fine foreign sports car. Not only is the initial investment high, but the monthly tune-ups are very expensive. How much money do you have for dog food? Don't laugh — it'll cost over a hundred dollars a year to feed a big dog.

The cost of a purebred dog might be the determining factor in deciding whether you want a pedigree or just dog-dog. But don't be fooled. You might as well get a good dog because no matter what you spend, $5 or $155 or better, the original investment is the smallest of your canine expenditures. Beware of bargain dogs if you're interested in blood lines and pedigrees. You get what you pay for. Which reminds me of the man who was shocked at the stiff price the kennel owner was asking for a pup. Not wishing to spend that much, he turned to his wife for support, asking what she thought. She said, "I think he's the cutest, most darling dog I've ever seen." "My dear," replied the husband, "are you helping *me* to buy or *him* to sell?"

Figure out if the dog's going to like you. Do you have the room to exercise him? A Chihuahua friend of mine has a master who drives a Volkswagen. The dog gets all the exercise he needs jumping around in the back seat. Try this on your Great Dane. Although a beagle is only fifteen inches high he should be on a rabbit trail, not following a mink on Madison Avenue. Don't try your apartment for size on a full-grown, high-strung Irish setter.

The real advantage of buying a registered dog is that when bought as a pup you know what he'll be like when he grows up. You're taking your chances with a mixed breed unless you know both parents; even then it's not always possible to estimate the pup's future appearance and temperament. A mixed-breed dog may have the physical characteristics of one of the parents and the nervous disposition of the other.

Disposition is of utmost importance in the selection of the family pet. The hereditary factors should be considered, though training at the right time, as we'll see later, has a major effect on molding the disposition of the dog.

Picking the breed is important. I have a friend who got a schnauzer for his wife. I told him I thought it was a good trade.

7

So, why start with strikes against you? Select from the list of dogs that are known to have friendly dispositions. Some breeds have become so popular that they're being bred for market purposes. Inbreeding produces high-strung nervous animals — they're not good around kids.

Here is a partial list of popular breeds that are good with children:

American water spaniel	coonhound	Labrador retriever
basset hound	Dalmatian	old English sheep dog
beagle	English setter	pointer
boxer	English shepherd	poodle
Brittany spaniel	foxhound	Saint Bernard
bulldog	Golden retriever	sheltie
collie	Irish water spaniel	springer spaniel

Dogs for one reason or another not good for children:

American cocker spaniel	Italian greyhound	Pomeranian
American toy fox terrier	Japanese spaniel	Samoyed
Chesapeake	Kerry blue terrier	Scotch terrier
Chihuahua	Malemute	spitz
chow	Maltese terrier	toy Manchester
dachshund	Mexican hairless	wire-haired fox terrier
Doberman pinscher	miniature pinscher	Yorkshire terrier
Husky	Pekingese	

There's a theory among some dog breeders that might be an old wives' tale, but it does seem to make sense. They speak of mid-European or German dogs as one-man, hardheaded animals who need a firm hand for training, and contrast this "Prussian" temperament to the English dogs that, much like the English people, are quiet, good-natured, and only fight when pushed into it . . . then they're scrappers. The English dogs make excellent pets for children.

It certainly is understandable that dogs would take on the character of the people, and that through generations of selective breeding the people would select the type of dog that fits their personality. You should do the same.

After you've come to your decision, stop in front of a mirror and take a look. Does the dog of your choice fit you? If you're in the 200-pound area and you're going to have a Pekingese, one or the other of you is going to look rather foolish . . . and I don't think it's going to be the dog.

Then there's the woman who didn't really mind what breed she got as long as it wasn't one of the hunting ones. She thought it was impolite to point.

The puppy comes home. Gretchen comes a-running. She jumps up and down with joy, claps her hands, throws off her coat. She plants a kiss on the pup, he plants one right back . . .

LET THE SURPRISE PACKAGE BE BROUGHT HOME

All right, so you didn't pick your Aunt Minnie. She came with the family. But at least be sure you pick your puppy; he's going to be with you for the next fifteen years. Don't make the error of letting the children in the family make the decision for you. They'll learn to love the dog of your choice as much as the one of their choice. The kids shouldn't even go to the kennel to do the picking. This is a job for adults. Let the surprise package be brought home.

Where you're going to buy your dog is really up to you. Try to determine the reputation of the people who are selling you the dog. It's much like buying anything else. If you're going to buy an automobile you want to know you're dealing with a reliable dealer. When you go to see the litter, look to see if the kennel is kept clean — whether it has a fresh odor — and note what condition the mother is in. Of course it's very important that you pick a dog you like, and there's always one that wins your heart. But be practical about it. Watch all the puppies play. Note their reactions to different situations. Stay away from the shy dogs, the listless puppies, or the nervous ones. It might be good, if it's practical for you, to visit the litter a couple of times. If all the puppies look alike put some fingernail polish on the toenails of the one you like so you'll be able to recognize him on your return visit.

... both Mother and Dad get bussed. Throughout the excitement Mother holds the dog. Pup
is having a tough day, no use making it worse. When things settle they can be introduced.

Examine the puppy's eyes. Are they clear? A discharge can spell real
trouble. A heavy discharge from the nose is also a serious problem with a
puppy. It can very easily mean distemper, the major killer of dogs. Examine
the rectum for any signs of diarrhea. Run your hand through the puppy's
hair. The puppy should be free from parasites and the skin should be soft
and pliable. The hair should be soft and have a good gloss to it. Watch the
puppy move around. Is he agile? If he is, he most likely has no nutritional
deficiencies. Turn him over, check the puppy's navel. A lump can mean an
umbilical hernia which can cause trouble later.

Teeth are important. He'll squawk, but lift his jowls and see that his
bite is even, that his teeth are regular, and that uppers and lowers fit in the
form of a good bite. Make sure the puppy's teeth are not stained brown, a
sure sign that the puppy had or has distemper. Check the gums to see that
they're pink and clear.

As you may have noted, we haven't explained to you how to buy an
older dog. We won't. Starting with a puppy and starting him at a specific
age is so essential to our new method of training that we won't tell you how
to select an older dog. Although it's much the same as getting a puppy, we
would like to impress upon you that to get the best out of a dog you must
start with a puppy, *and you must start the puppy at age 49 days* . . . this is
now scientific fact. Let me show you.

10

Chapter 3

The Dog's Mental Development
(a New Training Method)

For centuries, dogs have been trained under a theory that a one-year-old dog was like a seven-year-old boy ready for school; a two-year-old dog was likened to a fourteen-year-old, thus carrying this one-to-seven ratio throughout the dog's life until a seven-year-old dog was like a 49-year-old man . . . just going over the hill. Dog trainers are slowly starting to recognize that this is an old wives' tale. Scientists have shown that this seven-to-one ratio is only a *physical* comparison between man and dog and has nothing to do with the mental development of dogs. If you wait until a dog is a year old before he starts to train, you may have waited too long. This new information will be the foundation of the training of your dog.

Dr. J. Paul Scott, Director of the Animal Behavior Laboratory at Hamilton Station of the Roscoe B. Jackson Memorial Laboratory in Maine, directed the project that developed this new thesis. This information was derived while helping Guide Dogs for the Blind, Inc., in their dog training program.

Seeing Eye dogs receive the most rigorous and exact training of any dogs. For years it was believed that breeding was the answer to supplying puppies for this training. The breeding of the very finest Seeing Eye dogs produced litters of which only 20 per cent of the puppies had the ability, it seemed, to go through the rigid training to become Guide Dogs. In recent years the demand for these trained dogs has been greater than the supply. Dr. Scott and his team of workers sought and found the answer to the supply problem. It was a new approach to training. That new training method is *acceleration.*

Scientific study showed that there are five critical periods of a pup's life, five phases of his mental development. The shocking thing is that they all take place before the dog is sixteen weeks old. By this time the dog's brain has reached its adult form and size but, of course, without adult experience. So, instead of waiting for the puppy to grow up so it could be trained, Dr. Scott's works proved that it was actually harmful to delay. Starting the training early under the new accelerated program, the experimenters produced *90-per-cent success* in litters of the same breeding that produced only 20 per cent under the traditional methods of training. Many observers first thought that this outstanding success might be because of the exacting conditions of the scientific training procedures. When the accelerated training method was put into actual practice in Seeing Eye kennels and training programs, one full year's program even outstripped the laboratory results . . . 94 per cent of all litters successfully completed the rigorous training. This certainly is proof that early training can produce hitherto unbelievable results.

Let's take a look at the new findings about the mental make-up of the puppy and see how it will affect your training.

FIRST CRITICAL PERIOD — 0 TO 21 DAYS

Zero to 21 days is the first critical period. During these three weeks the pup's mental capacity is almost zero. The pup reacts only to its needs — warmth, food, sleep, and its mother. If anything at all could be taught, it would be strictly in the area of survival, such as a simple test of getting food. Abruptly on the 21st day his senses seem to function. He's like a house that's been built and wired for all the electrical appliances but has not been hooked up to the current. Then on the specific day the juice is applied and everything starts to function. In all breeds of dogs this happens on the 21st day of life. This leads immediately to the second critical period.

SECOND CRITICAL PERIOD — 21 TO 28 DAYS

The 21st to the 28th day is the time of the second phase — it's when the pup absolutely needs Momma. During this week the dog senses function, the brain and nervous system start to develop, and the big new world around him can be a pretty frightening experience. The emotional and social stress of life will have the greatest impact on him during this week. Removal from mother at this time could be drastic.

THIRD CRITICAL PERIOD — 28 TO 49 DAYS

From 28 to 49 days is the third period of development. Slowly the dog reacts to his surroundings. He ventures away from Mother to explore the world around him. It's at the end of this period that the dog's nervous system and his brain will have developed to the capacity of an adult but, of course, without the experience. He'll be ready to recognize people and respond to the voice. He'll have spent enough time in the litter to know that he's a dog. This may sound strange, but it has been shown that puppies taken from the litter too soon were difficult to breed later on. They just never got the idea that they were dogs. It's also during this third period that the social order or pecking order of the litter starts to form. This means the pups that learn to get in and fight for their food will tend to become bullies and the pups that are cowed by the more aggressive pups will become shy and develop wallflower personalities. It's desirable for the pup to live in the litter long enough for him to get a little competitive spirit from his family life, but too much is harmful. The puppy is now ready to learn, and learn he will, so it's better for you to get into the picture at this point and have him learn the things that will mold the type of personality that you want the dog to have.

Up until this time the dog was too young to take from the mother and could benefit from the social situation of the litter. But when *the dog is exactly 49 days old*, although he will be physically immature, his brain will have attained its full adult form.

FOURTH CRITICAL PERIOD — 49 TO 84 DAYS

The trainer and the dog should start to get to know each other *now*, not a week later or a week earlier. Dr. Scott's research has shown that this, the 49th day, is the best time in a dog's life to establish the dog-human relationship. The person who's going to train the dog will, in effect, now take the place of the pup's mother. Through feeding, playing, and general care of the dog at this age — seven to twelve weeks — a bond will be established that will have a permanent effect on the dog. At no later time in the dog's life will the pup have the ability to achieve as strong a bond or rapport with humans as at this age.

The research at the Behavior Laboratory showed that human contact in this seven- to twelve-week period is almost the whole key to the dog's future prospects. Puppies that were completely isolated for as little as the first sixteen weeks of life grew into dogs that were incapable of being trained, let alone becoming companion dogs.

Simple commands can be taught at this time. The teaching is at this

13

point in the form of games. There should be no discipline, and by the time the dog is twelve weeks old — the end of the preschool or fourth critical stage of his development — the dog will know what is meant by commands SIT, STAY, COME, and possibly HEEL.

Getting settled in the new home is a very important part of his education. A secure puppy will be a happy dog and will take to learning and discipline.

The new information has shown that dogs can get what is called kennel blindness. They just eat and sleep and exist, waiting for someone to come and plunk down some money in order to take them home. Dogs that have had absolutely no human contact before sixteen weeks of age have little chance of becoming what we want in a companion. Dogs that have missed human contact for even thirteen weeks, and who were bred to become working dogs, may be completely untrainable as workers.

One of the most interesting aspects of the Seeing Eye research was the information about interrupted training. Dogs started at a very early age, handled and trained through this fourth critical period — age twelve weeks — were then put back in the kennel situation. The lessons stopped for a period of only two weeks. After the two weeks, human contact and lessons were begun again, but only 57 per cent of these dogs were able to go on to become Guide Dogs. When the formal lessons and human contact were stopped for three weeks, only 30 per cent went on through the rigorous training to become Seeing Eye dogs. These facts dramatically show that to make the most out of a dog, the training has to begin early and without interruption and be carried into the last critical phase of the puppy's development.

FIFTH CRITICAL PERIOD — 84 TO 112 DAYS

This fifth period — from 84 to 112 days — is when the puppy starts to school. The play-teaching games stop and the formal lessons start. The dog is ready to learn *disciplined* behavior. This is the time a young dog will declare his independence. At this time, dog and trainer resolve the problem of who's going to be boss. Deciding who's boss can be settled if the dog is started late, but it might take a two-by-four to do it.

We prepare the dog for learning in the seven- to twelve-week period. Fundamental training then begins at twelve weeks, and by the end of sixteen weeks this dog will know his basic commands and respond well to them.

What we've tried to do with this scientific information is to put it in such a way as to relate it to the training of a house pet. So many people will say that they got their dog at six months, a year, or whatever, and declare what a fine pooch they have. What they say may be true, but they don't know how much better their dog could have been. By starting the dog with the family at the right age, you'll be taking the luck out of success.

HOW A DOG LEARNS

How does a dog learn? How does a child learn? In the last 40 years the teaching techniques in our schools have just about reversed themselves. The fad of progressive education is over. Professor John Dewey's dog would bark in his grave if he knew what they're now saying about his master's theories and philosophies which were the vogue among educators in the 1920's.

Children have been taught for thousands of years, but teachers still don't seem to agree on the best way to do it. You would think we could find the answer to such a basic problem with all the scientific information and techniques we have at hand today. But it's understandable. We can't make laboratory animals out of our kids, so we do the best we can with theories.

Dr. Scott's research in mental development, carried on under complete laboratory control, has come up with real answers for dogs. The key to his work — when to teach — gives us a new insight into how to teach. Handling the dog at such an early age automatically makes the learning process a way of life for the dog. This has been a real step forward in dog training; it has changed training techniques.

Work dogs — the hunting breeds — are now being handled and trained under this new system. For hundreds of years trainers advocated that dogs be started in their training at the age of six months to a year. Now we know that we can have dogs well trained to hunt by the time they're six months old.

The ancient adage, "You can't teach an old dog new tricks," was written by some old dog who was just trying to get out of work. True, an old dog that has learned nothing can learn nothing, but a dog that has learned to learn will continue to learn all his life.

Both kids and dogs start out with a strong desire to please. As a parent,

I sometimes wonder what happens to that desire. As a dog trainer, I find that a dog wants to please, all through his life. Some forward-thinking cave man threw some starving mutt a fat stewing bone — and for millions of years since, man has had a grateful friend who wants to serve by pleasing. This becomes one of the most valuable training tools we have.

A dog responds to his master's display of pleasure or displeasure. There's always tension in a learning situation. Reward reduces the tension and gives pleasure. Reprimand or punishment increases the tension and produces discomfort. The dog's instinctive desire to please leads him to seek your pleasure. He tries to do what you want in order to receive your good graces. This we call learning.

The stronger you can build the urge to please in the puppy, the easier the training job is going to be on both of you. When the puppy is started in his training at seven weeks, just the fact that we care for and love him at that early age intensifies the rapport between teacher and pupil. At first there is no reprimand in the training — training is in the form of fun games. This helps to build the desire to please. As he develops, common sense on your part will show the way to properly balance reward and punishment to keep the learning mechanism going.

A dog learns by association. The learning process is a matter of repetition, more repetition, and still more, until it becomes a part of the dog's behavior. We then call it memory.

Dogs can be taught on two levels of learning — the conscious and the unconscious level — according to what is being taught.

Learning on the unconscious level is the learning that the dog does without being aware that he's learning. The dog is repeatedly put into a situation; the situation is duplicated so many times that the dog comes to react in a predictable manner. There is no reprimand or reward; the dog just does what he's expected to do because he has never done it any other way.

Learning on the conscious level is when the dog knows that he's being taught something. This learning is done in the formal lessons and starts when the dog is twelve weeks old. The dog goes to school. Here is where common sense, love, affection, firmness, more firmness, and spankings are the teacher's devices.

You show the dog what you want. He finds out what your language means by trial and error. Once he has the idea, you put him through the action, give the command. He soon associates the action with the command. Then, by repetition you cement it all in his think-tank. Along the way in his training he'll try you for size to see what he can get away with. This is also part of learning.

Teaching a puppy is just like a kid building with blocks. The kid builds block by block until the whole thing falls down because of a mistake. So he starts over from the beginning, eventually learning that he can build higher by making the foundation stronger. So the puppy learns: first SIT, then STAY, then COME. When he goofs on COME start him over with SIT, then STAY. He'll finally learn COME, but in the meantime the repetition of the things he knows, SIT and STAY, make them firmly understood upstairs.

The good part about all this training is that the trainer doesn't have to be smart. I've seen some rather sad humans train some smart dogs. It's not like teaching a kid geometry — to teach that you have to be able to do it yourself. To teach a dog to fetch you don't have to be able to do it, and if you're an adult and you do, you're going to look rather foolish.

It's not 100% necessary to show a dog how to do everything expected of him. Something's . . .

THE TEACHING ROLE

"Beware of Dog" signs should be taken seriously by trespassers and trainers. A smart dog will take advantage of the teacher. A dog is just as keen at "feeling out" in a training situation as you ought to be. He knows that he's supposed to react to the lessons with the wag of the tail. He's quick to try putting on a sad look, a put-on pose hoping that you'll melt and stop the lesson. If you do he's got you and he'll start training you. He's just hoping that you'll decide that he's a sensitive puppy. I've seen so many dogs go untrained because the owner got the feeling the puppy wasn't mature enough for schooling. People forget that learning is never easy and the only way to be successful as a trainer is to keep the pupil-teacher relationship rigid while school is in session. Always win your point while training; you must retain the authority at all times. The way is easy; if you use firmness sprinkled with affection, the dog will soon learn that he can't evade his lessons.

. . . gone wrong teaching fetch. Instead, Tar learns to bite the tail of the hand that feeds him.

HOW TO DEVELOP CONFIDENCE

A dog has to learn to have confidence in you. We began to earn the confidence of the puppy when we took him out of his litter at seven weeks of age. The trainer is now the mother, and as mother you have the opportunity and the responsibility of molding the desired personality in the dog. This is one of the main reasons for taking the dog from the litter at seven weeks.

As the training schedule begins the dog will respond to the trainer's demands. It's important here to be consistent. Don't be changeable. Make sure the dog knows what's expected of him and of you or you'll undermine all the good you have accomplished by starting early.

Dogs are very practical and have no moral sense. They'll use any method that will achieve what *they* want. Children will do the same thing. If a dog learns that he can get what he wants by whimpering and whining, he'll do it. If he gets the attention he needs by barking, he'll bark. It's very important to teach a dog from the beginning that there's a right and a wrong way to do things. The right way will get him your pleasure. If he insists on doing things the wrong way make darn sure that he knows that he's heading for trouble.

To continue to build confidence throughout the training, make sure the dog knows what was expected of him in the particular situation before you reprimand him. Make sure he knows why he's being punished. A young dog has practically no memory, so you have to be Johnny-on-the-spot with the reprimand. Simple lapses can shatter confidence.

One evening at dinner a friend was telling me the problems he was having training his very nervous poodle. While stating the facts, the dog came over, sat by his side. The dog went over to him because the dog's name was used in the conversation. The master noticed this and stopped talking and offered the dog a piece of meat from the table in spite of strict rules against this. The dog took it, hurried to the other side of the room, then ate it. It was quite obvious that he was trained not to eat from the table — that's why he took the meat across the room. The rule was changed on this occasion at the master's discretion. When this inconsistency was pointed out, the trainer said he never thought of it that way. He figured he was being extra kind to the dog. On further talking, we found other areas in the training where the master was inconsistent.

Of course this dog was nervous; he didn't know how to respond to the training. He wasn't sure how the teacher was going to teach or how the teacher was going to respond. Security is a most important trait to develop. Inconsistency will undermine confidence.

SOME WORDS ABOUT REPRIMAND

Almost every book you read will have a different approach. Some books say never, but never, hit a dog. One book says never lay a hand on a dog unless he's going to bite someone. It's too late then, as far as I'm concerned. A dog should never be allowed to get that far before he feels the sting of a spanking. Which reminds me of the beggar who approached a man walking his dog and said, "Excuse me, sir, I haven't had a bite in weeks" — you know what happened.

Some object to spanking the dog, thinking he'll become hand-shy. This won't happen if you handle it correctly. A dog doesn't resent a spanking if he knows he's done wrong. He'll learn that the hand that cares for him, feeds him, and pats him when he's obedient is the same hand that stings him when he becomes obstreperous.

Some suggest the rolled newspaper. In my opinion this is very cruel. It's wrong to teach a dog to fear a loud noise. A dog can be conditioned this way and end up a nervous wreck. Reprimand has to be given immediately, not after the act and after you go find where you left your rolled-up newspaper. Also, is it any wonder why postmen and paperboys get the seats of their pants taken out?

There's a wide difference between dog lovers and dog trainers. A trainer can accomplish two things — love his dog and have a well-behaved and trained companion. Dog lovers accomplish only one thing. People seem to forget that love alone will produce a spoiled dog . . . discipline by the hand on the rump can be an act of love.

LET'S DEFINE REPRIMAND

Everyone knows how to love a dog; a pat, a caress, a few kind words — they eat it up. But the reprimand is quite tricky. Almost from the moment the dog enters his new home with you he's going to hear one command and he'll continue to hear it the rest of his life. . . . It's the command NO. The whole purpose of training is to diminish the use of this command. By the time the puppy is an adult he'll know what's expected of him and the command will very seldom be necessary.

Reprimand can take many forms and degrees. It doesn't mean only the act of laying a leash across his back. You can hurt a dog just as much by completely ignoring him. For example, if you're teaching him STAY and instead he COMES, he'll expect a pat and a kind word. Don't give him the time of day. Take him back to where he was, start him over. Ignoring him hurts his pride.

A dog instinctively recognizes a threatening gesture. If you're sure that he knows what's expected but suspect that he's just testing you, come at him with an upraised hand. The dog's just trying to assert his independence; this is not a thrashing offense. Here's where you have to use your judgment. Consider the degree of the offense. I usually use my hat as the threatening weapon. This approach will make him fold . . . he'll come around. Take into account the circumstances, the age of the dog, and whether he should have known better — then mete out the punishment.

When he becomes downright ornery and stubborn there's only one way to straighten him out. Heaven protect me from the SPCA, but I'm going to say it. Thrash the dog. Do it with fervor, but with intelligence. I clip the dog with the folded leash until he cries out once. I talk angrily and make a big fuss while I swing and continue to speak in a firm tone after the outcry to be sure it registered. Then I switch over to a pleasant tone of voice and begin the lessons all over again. It's very important to get the situation back to normal as quickly as possible. Don't nag. This clean-cut discipline isn't cruel, as some think. It's kind. Failure to discipline is crueler.

IT AIN'T WHAT YOU SAY, IT'S THE WAY THAT YOU SAY IT

Every schoolboy knows that the same words can mean opposite things with different inflections. WOW, when spoken quickly with an upward inflection, means . . . she's 38-24-38. WOW, with a downward intonation and drawn out, means not so hot. WOW, drawn out and a slight upward inflection, expresses astonishment.

Dogs become masters at interpreting the voice. They never understand our language as we know it; they work mainly from the tone of the words. You can scold a dog by harshly telling him you love him. A dog has very sensitive ears and he's irritated by harsh high-pitched tones. Keep your voice down in low conversational tones. The tone can encourage a puppy, but don't beg a dog to respond to a command. There's no place for baby talk in training. It's a command you're giving, not a request, so speak with authority.

A young puppy will try you out by puttering around before he starts to respond to your command. He's just stalling for time and trying to see how much he can get away with. Show him with a good rousing *"Hey you! What's going on?"* It'll straighten him out.

There are only about ten words that your dog's going to learn, but he'll learn hundreds of intonations.

The commands should be short, brisk, single words like SIT, STAY, COME, NO. Don't add a lot of gibberish to the commands. Don't say, "SIT, boy, come on now ... SIT, fellow ... no, no, let's try it again. Over here now, Beau, SIT." A dog's just going to get confused with all your complicated language. In that example, we were asking the dog to do one thing — SIT ... but if you go back over that language you'll see that four commands were given — SIT, NO, COME, BEAU. His name is really a command for attention.

While on the subject of names, give the dog a snappy, short, one-syllable call-name: Jack, Bell, Jed, Jing. The name shouldn't sound like one of the commands: Beau or Bo is too close to NO. The dog could get confused. Leave the fancy names on the pedigree.

I know one family who had a fine French poodle pup and changed her name right in the middle of her training. Daughter named the pup; what could be a more appropriate name than Marie Antoinette? That puppy's name was changed as of the first Sunday morning that she was old enough to be put out the front door to do her business. Marie Antoinette decided that she was old enough to do a little investigating. When Father, still in pajamas, went out on the porch to call the wanderer home, he raised his voice with all his power and bellowed over the quiet Sunday landscape: "Marie Antoinette ... MARIE ANTOINETTE ... COME HOME!" One of his unappreciative neighbors, roused out of his sleep, hung his sleepy head out the window and in a falsetto voice called back: "I'll be right there."

Gretchen's pal Jeremy is afraid of Tar. She shows him how to approach from underneath . . .

SHOW YOU'RE A FRIEND

In spite of thousands of years of domestication, dogs still have retained most of their primeval instincts; man has lost most of his. Man has come to depend on language for most of his communication; dogs use all their senses. I've heard an old dog trainer say, "One thing dogs and women have in common, they know your true feelings, no matter what you say." A dog will instinctively try to sense your attitude and respond accordingly. If he's not sure, he'll be cautious. It's said that if you're afraid, a dog can smell your fear.

In conducting the lessons, your stance, body position, and movements will have a lot to do with the way the dog will respond. A dog instinctively doesn't like to be towered over. Standing upright doesn't appear to be a very friendly attitude on your part; bend over when you give the commands. The dog will respond with enthusiasm. Even a youg pup understands this. From across a room or a yard, say nothing to the puppy; just get down on all fours and watch him run to you.

Movements must be slow and deliberate, never quick and jerky. If a correction is to be made, move in slowly and start the lesson over from the beginning. Children will have to be warned not to lurch for a puppy to make a correction.

Children, and even adults, should learn to approach a strange dog by bending over and meeting the dog on his level. Let the dog come to you, and if the hand is going to be extended it shouldn't be over the dog's head, but under his chin. Once the dog sees that everyone is going to be friendly

... Let him smell your hand. Don't make loud noises; move your hand slowly. Fast friends.

he'll be friendly too; then you can pat him on top of the head. A dog feels that the hand over his head is a threat.

START 'EM YOUNG ... WITH THE RIGHT HABITS

The long-time sports editor for International News Service, Lawton Carver, tells this story about a mutual dog-training friend Gene Hill. Gene had gotten two new possessions: a new bird-dog pup and a new car. Gene was driving the editor, Carver, out to his farm to see how the pup would work on game birds. Between demonstrations of what the car would and wouldn't do, Gene talked dog training. He bent Lawton's ear about dogs being creatures of habit: "If you start 'em young with the right habits half the training problem is solved," the trainer said. As he drove along, he took out a cigarette, lit it with a match, lowered the window, threw out the match, and went on with his monologue. Lawton interrupted him and pointed out that man also sure was a creature of habit. Here Gene had a new car with a new cigarette lighter and he didn't use it. The trainer, not to be interrupted, went on with his discussion, took out another cigarette, reached for the new lighter, lit the cigarette, lowered the window ... of course you know what he threw out.

Planning the habits that are going to become the adult dog's way of life is important right from the beginning. You should decide right from the start if you're going to allow your dog to get up on the furniture, beg at the table, sit in your lap, sleep on your bed, and bother your guests. You'll have

24

no problem if you decide which of these activities you don't want and never let 'em start. But a puppy is so cute. People tend to let the new member of the family do anything while he's very small, then wonder why they have difficulty later. Take the extra work out of learning — develop good habits early.

In training working dogs, habits are developed in the puppy from the very first lessons. For example, command COME is taught to a hunting dog so that he'll respond in three different ways: voice, hand signal, and whistle. Having the family dog COME to whistle can be very useful. This refinement in training is a very simple thing to accomplish. Every time the training situation for teaching COME is set up, and a vocal command is given, blow four fast blasts on the whistle. In a week even a very young puppy will come to either the voice command or the whistle, whichever you wish. The advantage here is that a whistle can be heard half a mile or more.

He learns this by habit, the same as he learns not to beg at the table. It's just as important not to allow bad habits to get started as it is to encourage good ones. Unlearning bad habits and relearning good ones is very confusing to a dog. Remember, you can't reason with a dog; it's going to be hard for him to understand that you're changing your mind.

It's important that all members of the family understand just what is and what isn't allowed. Youngsters who train get pleasure seeing to it that the puppy doesn't break the rules of the house. It seems to give the kid a sense of responsibility, and it's a pleasure to a kid not to always be on the receiving end of commands.

Politely correct any guests that allow the puppy to break the house rules. Maybe this guest likes having the puppy in his lap, but your next guest might be in satin.

DON'T NAG THE DOG TO DEATH

A dog isn't like a new electrical appliance that'll work every time you flick a switch. Some folks never seem to give the dog a moment's peace while they're training him. If he walks around they tell him to STAY. If he leaves the room Fido's given the command COME. If he wags his tail for attention he's told to SIT. If he barks for attention he's told QUIET. Don't constantly train the dog. Let him enjoy life and the things he knows how to do. Don't bore him with his work — you'll do more harm than good.

After a dog has been in training for a while it will seem that he's making no progress. Children have this same pattern of learning. The learning is fun for a while, but the whole thing just becomes a bloody bore. Try to recognize this. It's sometimes hard to distinguish between boredom and stubbornness. He may not be bored at all but expressing his independence and showing you who's going to be the boss.

If he's bored, let up on the training, or for a day or so have him do only those things he likes to do. It's important that the trainer doesn't break the dog's spirit.

If you think he's expressing his independence, be cautiously firm. Win each battle slowly, but not harshly . . . you only want to *teach* him who's boss, not *show* him.

Although it's possible to train too much, it's never possible to play too much.

SOME MORE THINGS

What's the first thing you do after Thanksgiving dinner? . . . Sleep. To a dog every meal is Thanksgiving. Don't try to train him after he has eaten. He'll be slow and sluggish. I like to have class just before meals. Not only is the dog alert, but the meal will be part of the reward.

Have no distractions during the lessons. Work alone with the pup. Don't have an audience. If an adult is helping a child, the adult should stay in the background as much as possible after the child gets the hang of what's expected. We have a neighbor's cat that drives me crazy when I work with a puppy. The cat loves dogs and continually teases the puppy when school is in session by dashing out from under bushes. That cat even has the length of the leash figured out. When such an interruption occurs there's only one solution — close school for the day.

How will you know when you're going too far? Some trainers suggest training by the clock, ten minutes. I do it by the tail. The tail is a very good indicator of a dog's attitude. A high tail means he's still with you. A low tail means he's had it for the day.

Some days a dog will be more receptive to school than on others. After ten minutes or so if he wants to keep going, if he's still enthusiastic, continue. The important thing here is to judge the dog's progress by the indicators: his tail, his enthusiasm, his response. They show you how fast you can advance your dog from lesson to lesson. As he gets older his mental endurance will increase.

Learn to anticipate what your dog is going to do. This will take a lot of frustration out of the yard training for both of you. For example, when a pup is held by command in the SIT, STAY position, he, of course, will want to break and come to you. After he has held it for a short period, but just can't stand it any longer, he'll give a warning by a slight body movement that he is about to break. Anticipate this — command COME just before he breaks. Now he has done two things correctly instead of one thing incorrectly. The lesson continues in a happy mood.

Try to end school each day on a good note. If he's not progressing on the latest lesson to your satisfaction, the last command should be something he already knows well. Then you can ring the bell, close up school for the day, and give the pup some loving. Tomorrow is another day.

AND FINALLY — KIDS AND DOGS

After one year of married life most couples either have a baby or a dog. If it's the baby that comes first, that just postpones the dog a few years. They eventually get around to the four-legged baby. I once heard an old farmer say, "There just ain't much difference, 'cept one's got a tail."

Puppies, human or dog, seem to understand each other. They are made of the same material. I won't state which is smarter — I might be prejudiced. They have a rapport that only they understand. They think alike, act alike, train alike, and can outsmart adults in like manner.

If the dog puppy came into the home before the human one, it will be only fair to keep the dog in mind when the infant screams for lunch. Up until this time the dog received all the attention. He was king. He'll become jealous when given a back seat — all of a sudden someone else is getting the attention he once got and there is no way to prepare him in advance. When you make a fuss over baby you should also talk to the dog; he'll understand more than the baby anyway. Make the dog feel important; a pat won't hurt. Show him he's still on the in, in spite of the screaming newcomer. Have a tidbit for him when you feed baby — make him feel he's still part of the family. The dog will learn to accept baby in a very short time, and it won't be too long before they're kennel mates.

Some years ago it was a well-known story around town that that certain sports editor for I.N.S., Lawton Carver, presented his eighteen-minute-old son with a $100 Orvis fly rod. A few years later when we were on a fishing trip together — and he was using a fly rod inscribed Lawton Carver, Jr. — he told me that he had been tempted then to make the gift a dog but one of the nurses was a holy terror and wouldn't let him bring a dog into the hospital.

Parents can be in for a real shock when they give their little darling a puppy. A young child will mirror the type of training he has received and will handle the puppy much the way he has been handled. I don't mean if a child shows some minor cruelty to the pup that he has learned that from Mom. All children are born with some of the devil in them; getting rid of the devil is part of growing up.

One family I know had their eyes opened when the daughter was continually observed screaming at the dog, shaking him rather hard when he would not "obey." They were just smart enough to recognize the fact that she was training the way she was being trained. That dog turned out pretty good — they all changed their methods.

The child has to be taught from the very beginning that the puppy is just as much of a playmate as the kids next door. Teach the child that the puppy has rights and even property and should not be teased. Teach him to play nicely with the puppy or puppy, too, may lose his temper.

When a child is able to reason with you, even though he might be wrong, he'll be old enough for a dog. Gretchen (in these pictures) was six-and-a-half when she got her Labrador retriever. She was able to understand that a puppy's tail was not his leash, and that a wag of the tail had to be earned.

"You're not really considering sending me off to school yet. I'm only eight weeks old."

Chapter 4

Kindergarten — the Aspects of Early Learning

There's no more graphic way of showing training than by photographs, except possibly if I came out to your house. In Part I we presented the new theories of how a dog learns. Now, in Part II, we photographically document the development, the learning and teaching methods.

We buy the puppy and bring him home at the beginning of the fourth critical period of his learning; half of your success is assured by just taking the puppy home at this time and being kind to him. The other half that guarantees a successful final product is preparing the puppy to accept learning as a way of life.

Scientists have discovered by intelligence tests that no one particular breed of dog or any one dog in a litter is smarter than any other. What they've found is this: that the dog that takes responsibility faster learns better. And taking responsibility has to be learned.

The puppy starts kindergarten at seven weeks of age. For the next five weeks he gets this preschool training.

During the first five weeks of kindergarten we'll put him in the right environment and develop in him a sense of security. The mild restrictions and irritations that we impose on him will be to develop his tolerance. We'll set up play games, and we'll teach him specific simple commands, but most important will be the human contact he'll get during this whole period. During this preschool time we're molding the personality of the dog, we're building the foundations of a well-balanced dog. While doing these, we'll be showing you how to handle the dog and how to train him.

THE ONE-ROOM SCHOOLHOUSE

Set up shop in one room — the kitchen. Don't give the puppy the run of the "new big kennel." In his first home pup lived with his brothers and sisters in rather close quarters; living was rather simple. It will be best to start him off in your house the same way. He'll like it better, and so will you.

The length of time that he's confined here depends on how fast he learns a few simple facts of life. Puppies are very democratic and will just as soon soil an Oriental rug as make a biological comment on Red Smith's column in the New York *Herald Tribune*. We'll discuss this further when we talk about housebreaking.

We want the dog to feel secure in the new surroundings right from the beginning. It's really the best room in the house for him. It's the most active room. He won't feel lonely here. It has the nicest smells of all the rooms and it's easy to keep clean. There's not much in the kitchen that can be damaged at puppy level and not much at this level that can hurt the puppy.

With a screen blocking the doorway, kitchen also serves as a playpen. Mother can now keep an eye on both dog and kid puppies to see that they don't get too rough with each other.

One corner of the room will be made into the bedroom. This area should be free from drafts. A dog can stand cold but not drafts. The bed can be an old rug, a few old towels, a cloth bag filled with wood chips (preferably cedar), or a covered foam-rubber mat. But it won't make any difference to the pup — he'll be asleep quite a lot the first month.

Like any little boy, the quickest way to a puppy's heart is through his stomach. First thing in the new home feed him. He should've traveled from the kennel on an empty stomach.

Mother feeds puppy a biscuit before she turns on the noisy dishwasher. Giving him something he likes teaches him that noises won't hurt. Frightened dogs are shy and hard to train.

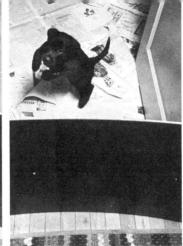

Block off the kitchen with a high board. Sometimes he thinks the new big kennel is a jail . . .

. . . But, it's really the best room. Someone is usually there, it's warm, it has the best of smells, good for a fast shut-eye and a fine field for playing ball. The puppy is isolated from other dogs until the proper time for his inoculations. They will protect him from distemper.

HOW TO PICK UP A PUPPY

Part of the sense of security that a puppy establishes is based on how people handle him. So, right from the beginning the kitchen is also schoolroom for Gretchen. So often in a learning situation a first experience is a lasting one. If the first experience isn't good it takes much work to correct the bad impression. Puppies can become man-shy if they're handled too

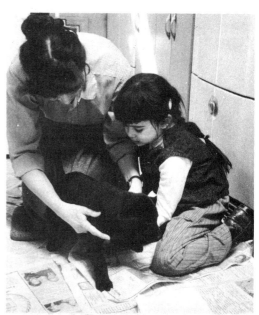
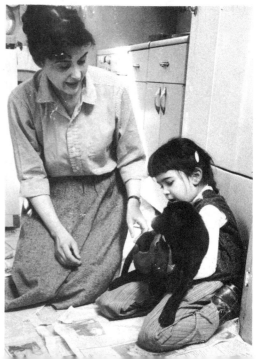

Mother shows her (above) how to support the pup. Then she tries it. The hands go underneath his hind quarters and his chest and hold his legs. Never pick a dog up by his limbs, his belly or the scruff of the neck. This is the very first time that Gretchen held Tar. Note her expressions, first watching then trying and finally the feeling of satisfaction. Gretchen is so pleased to have learned this. At first she was a little skeptical.

roughly at a young age.

Young children get a great delight out of holding a puppy in their arms. I think it's their way of playing mother. Puppies don't mind this if it's not done too much. I learned something here, too. Note the gloves on Gretchen. The first thing puppy did was to nip her finger. Gloves were her idea . . . and a good one.

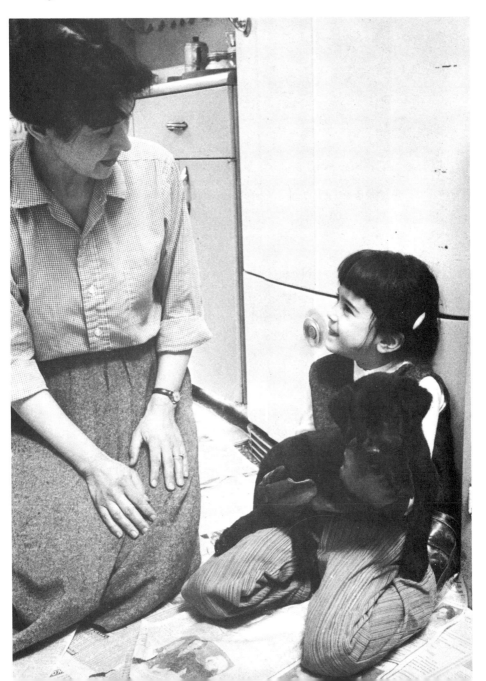

A puppy, just like a child, will gather his own possessions. Tar makes his first mistake. Old boots or shoes are a bad idea. He won't be able to differentiate between old ones and new ones. Teach him from the start what he may and may not have. His toys should be hard rubber, not soft rubber. Toys kill many pups. Don't let him have things he can tear up and eat. They love to chew. A happy pup will play by himself; he's emotionally secure.

SECURITY — THEY NEED THE FEELING, TOO

Professional dog breeders and trainers are often heard to say, "Oh, a fine puppy, very well bred, but a little sensitive." Sensitive, my eye. That pup is insecure; it's scared to death of its own shadow. Trainers will also talk of strong-headed pups that need a firm hand. Secure dogs neither have to win battles nor be afraid. Sensitive or hardheaded dogs are undesirable; in either case the dogs became what they were through their experiences — they weren't born that way. Both cases can be avoided.

It's obvious that in the first case the sensitive puppy lived too long with its littermates and was beaten up too often; in the second case the headstrong puppy or the bully was the pup that won all the fights in the litter and got all the food.

We now know why dogs develop different personalities. By removing the pup from its litter at seven weeks and then providing him with all his needs, protecting him from harm, making the new home a pleasant one, we'll make him a secure puppy. A secure puppy is a happy pup. A happy puppy will take to his lessons easily.

GO TO BED — IT'S FOR SLEEPING, NOT HOWLING

When the family retires, the pup retires . . . you hope. Lead him to his bed, command GO TO BED. Check to see that all the things that are supposed to be out of his reach are put up. Legs of chairs make delicious midnight snacks for young pups. Let him take a toy to bed (not a hard one that he can clank around the kitchen all night), turn out the lights, close the door, and cross your fingers. If you have the swinging-type kitchen door put a chair against it; otherwise he might push it open and get his head caught.

Some people suggested giving the dog an alarm clock or a hot water bottle to sleep with. Our results with that procedure have been a broken clock and a leaky water bag. There's no substitute for his being lonely. You might as well get used to the idea of a few bad nights' sleep. Both of you.

A little quiet loving instead of rowdy play before bedtime will help quiet him down. His last feeding should be close to bedtime or you can try a little warm milk. A box cut out in front will give him an extra sense of security; it will prevent midnight drafts.

The first rule is don't go in the kitchen to him. That's what he wants you to do. Let him howl it out. He must learn that his crocodile tears aren't going to soften you up. If he keeps it up, command QUIET through the door. It will help relieve your 3:30 A.M. nerves and will let the dog know that he's really not alone. If he continues to carry on, rap on the door and in a firm voice tell him "Quiet in there." Stand by the door. When he thinks you've gone he'll start up again. Say nothing, rap on the door hard . . . startle him.

The first few nights are the worst. After that he may try a few ineffectual howls for effect. He's just hoping there's an outside chance that you'll renege. Don't! Have a little patience here. Try a sleeping pill on yourself and try to be human next morning at breakfast.

HUMAN CONTACT

These pictures remind me of the Broadway musical hit song, "Getting to Know You." The scientists call it socialization, and it's the most important aspect of this kindergarten or preschool training. It's absolutely essential that a good rapport take place between the pup and the trainer at this age. This is when the strongest bond starts to form. The trainer should be the one who feeds the dog because whoever takes the place of the dog's mother will become very important to the dog. At this age the puppy will form a natural attachment to the one who cares for and instructs him.

This is the first time Tar and Gretchen played together. Right off, Tar scratched Gretchen on the face. He didn't mean it and to prove it he dragged her by the pigtail. This might be referred to as the first bond between child and dog. This is sure better than sitting alone in some kennel. As young as Tar is, he is ready to learn, so say the scientists. Dog trainers have noted that work dogs and hunting dogs learn faster if they live in the house and get human contact.

Enough is enough, so Gretchen tries another tactic. Those gloves sure were a good idea. He can't hurt them so she offers Tar a bite. She learns in seconds that Tar likes the taste of pigtails better than gloves. Mother stepped in, stopped the roughhouse. She explained to Gretchen that this wasn't the right kind of play. They should never play tug of war. Tar should be discouraged from pulling and hauling. It might seem cute now but not so cute later when he weighs ninety pounds. Turn the page, see a game that's good fun for all.

Show the pup the soft doll. Talk to him, shake the toy. If you get all excited he will too . . .

CANINE CONTACT

We've talked much about the contact of dogs with humans. It's just as important to get the child really interested in the dog. This will take place naturally when we show the child how to get the dog to respond to simple commands.

While we're preaching patience with the dog, remember to save some for your youngsters. Training is only a matter of communicating, and a child

. . . The trick is to get him back. Call him in a friendly tone, clap to get his attention . . .

. . . Throw it out when you think he's anxious enough. Point to it, tell him to go fetch . . .

is only in the learning process himself. The parent will have to stay one chapter ahead of both dog and child and direct things. Just as the dog needs encouragement by a pat on the head, so does the child. The real reward for the child will be the correct response from the dog. It's going to be the job of the parent to show the child exactly how to train, what to say, when to say it, the tone of voice to use, how to set up the learning situation.

. . . Praise him, he'll love it. If he tires don't force him to play if he doesn't want to.

Gretchen "suffers" along with her friend, all dressed up in his new collar and no place to go but the kitchen. Only have him wear it for an hour or so at a time. He'll scratch and maybe whimper while dragging the leash. He'll learn (right) to make the best of a bad situation.

43

PUTTING UP WITH IRRITATIONS

In spite of one of Al Jolson's old songs entitled, "Life Is Just a Bowl of Cherries," the sooner a puppy finds out that "Ain't Necessarily So" the happier he's going to be in this great, big, tough world. Learning to put up with mildly irritating situations, coping with them without sulking, will make pup a cooperative student.

After the puppy has had a few days to get acclimated put a collar on him for a short time each day. He'll scratch at it, but before long he'll get used to it, just like Papa got used to a necktie. If you start him early he won't fight it so much. By the time the pup has the run of the house and isn't living on a newspaper floor, attach the leash to the collar and let him drag it around behind him. He'll chew on it, scratch, play with it, but will soon ignore it. Let the child play with him while he has this paraphernalia on; soon he'll get the idea that these are his clothes, and being dressed is just a part of life. But impress upon your child that he's not to fool with the leash, just let it drag.

The leash will become a very important training tool. It should be lightweight and at least six feet long. It'll come to mean control to the dog. Very often a trained dog, who is acting just a little stubborn, will come around and behave when the leash is shown to him. I wish it were that easy at times with my kids.

Now he can go out, Gretchen decides to dress him for the occasion. So, he doesn't have . . .

. . . the right figure. Any boy dog who puts up being dressed like a girl learns tolerance.

MORE IRRITATIONS

Playing puppy's games, with all his nipping, can become rather irritating to Gretchen, so now Tar plays her game. Playing dolls is annoying, but it won't hurt him and Gretchen's having loads of fun.

ACCEPTING RESTRICTIONS

Putting certain restrictions on the pup will keep him from becoming a spoiled brat. Between the ages of seven and twelve weeks the dog must learn that you mean what you say. If he learns that he can get around you by barking or whining he'll work you as hard as he can.

A puppy can be very demanding on your time if you let him. He wants your attention, just like a child. He must learn that there are going to be times to eat, sleep, romp by himself, play with others, and go to school. It's important that he learn that he's not the one to decide when these things take place.

There are two ways to teach these restrictions. One, the puppy is put into a situation where he finally teaches himself. The second way he learns is to give him mild reprimands; he'll want to please you so much that you'll be surprised at how fast he gets the idea.

When we were talking about giving the dog security we explained why we take the puppy out of the litter situation when we do. By removing the pup from the litter and being kind, we can prevent the wallflower personality from developing. But all kindness and no restraint outside the litter and the dog can still develop a spoiled-brat or bully personality. Hardheaded dogs don't accept training easily. They make problems that wouldn't exist if they were taught at the crucial time of development to accept discipline and restriction.

It's unfair to the dog not to teach him what he can and can't do to get along and fit in with all the members in the house.

47   **At meal time Tar was always under foot. He wanted to play, Mother wanted to work. He must learn we do things when we want. This mild restriction teaches him he doesn't get his way . . .**

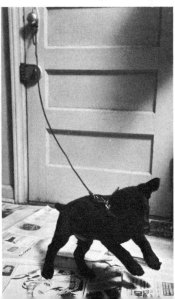

Teach the command QUIET. Firmly take his snout in your left hand, command QUIET. Squeeze his cheeks against his teeth, shake your finger at him. Use a rough tone of voice and the next time cuff him across the nose. You shouldn't completely suppress his desire to bark, but he should stop on command. Dogs are inclined to bark at doorbells, phones, dogs or people passing on the street. For the dog not within reach be ready with a piece of chain or three tin cans strung together. This is discussed in full on page 116. When he barks throw it on the floor near him, it'll scare him quiet. He's old enough now to learn this simple command. Since it's vital to his mental development that he learn some elementary lessons during this five-week period, it's vital to your mental health that he learn QUIET, fast.

. . . no matter how he barks, whines or jumps to get free. He'll soon learn that all the ruckus gets him naught. Might just as well lie down, take it easy, that's what a tied leash means.

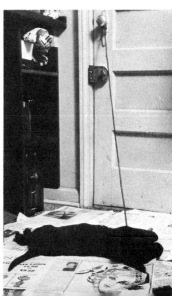

Show him his mistake, the puddle he made . . .   . . . Shake your finger and firmly scold him . . .

HOUSEBREAKING

Housebreaking means different things to different people. To the second-story man it means getting in. To the owner of a new puppy it means getting him out.

Of course housebreaking starts in the kitchen. A good heavy covering of newspaper in the kitchen will be the diaper for two weeks.

This housebreaking routine is not as bad as it sounds. Many people shy from getting young puppies because of the inconvenience of these few weeks. You're taking more of a chance and could end up with more serious problems by getting an older housebroken dog in order to avoid this training. Actually, a puppy does pretty well on this score. It takes a human puppy two years to be housebroken; a dog will learn what's expected in a few weeks and be able to control himself by the time he's four months old.

Here's a tip about drinking water. There's no reason to leave water down all day for the young puppy. Besides the liquid in his food, water should be given after each meal. The consistency of the last meal at night

...Catch him immediately, tell him he's bad...   ...BAD! He understands, so does Gretchen...

... After reprimanding, change the subject. Get things back so everybody's in a happy mood. You must catch the puppy right after his mistake or he won't remember or understand you.

should be rather dry. He'll be getting enough water and this system will help in his toilet training.

Paper-breaking is the first step. Since he'll just go where and when the urge happens to come, the whole kitchen is covered with paper. In a day or so you'll note that he seems to like a certain spot best. Remove only the soiled top layer of papers in the area he seems to like; leave some of the underlayers that still have the scent. When he shows consistent signs of sniffing around before he relieves himself on the favorite newspaper area, you can start diminishing the area covered by papers. Learning what the paper is for will take about a week. We've had some dogs learn it in three days and some in three weeks. Once he learns it you'll have a very small paper area to worry about. For working people who leave a dog all day in an apartment, this method becomes an emergency standby, even when the dog is an adult. Many people like to keep their dogs paper-trained so that they can travel easier with the pet.

Some like to start the puppy outdoors immediately. The theory is that if the dog gets used to the grass and trees he'll learn to prefer them. This is true, but wrong procedure. A seven-week-old puppy must be quarantined until your veterinarian tells you he's safe from distemper. This is discussed in full in Part III on dog care.

Once the quarantine is over we want the outdoor theory to take over. The dog should go outdoors after each meal. Those who live in the suburbs or country can put the dog on a run; those in the city will have to walk their pet. In either case, the dogs will most likely come back to the house, rush for the kitchen, and use the paper with a sigh of relief. Now what?

I have a friend living in an apartment who finally convinced his wife that they should have a dog. The bargain they made was that if he wanted a hunting dog he would have to housebreak it. I told him about the paper routine and things were going well. When the dog was down to a very small paper area it was time for curb training. Every night he walked the dog for hours without success. Finally, tired from a hard day in the office and a long hike each night, he would shuffle up to their fifth-floor walk-up where the dog would make a pee-line for the papers. After a week of this the wife complained that she never saw him, and when she did he was exhausted. He phoned me for help.

Saving the marriage was easy. "Take a piece of scented newspaper down to the curb," I told him. "In five minutes you'll be back mixing a drink for your wife."

"You know better!" This is one re-striction we insist you learn, NOW!

Take advantage of this situation. This is the best time to send the rugs out for a cleaning. You can have them stored for a month or so.

Of course a dog is going to make mistakes. You have to be Johnny-on-the-spot. If you see he's about to or has begun the accident, shout NO, grab him, and rush him to the papers. Don't rub the dog's nose in the mess as some trainers suggest — it won't do any good, and it's rather disgusting. What you have to do here is to catch the dog in the act and startle him. Speak very harshly to him. Of course, when he does the right thing plenty of praise in a friendly tone will get your point across.

It's a good idea to keep the papers down while in the process of outside training until the dog is old enough to have control over his bowels. Paper is left down at night and for accidents during the day.

When the dog is four months old you can try him with all papers up. You'll have to watch him very carefully. Actually, I see no reason to force the issue too soon. Although you can do it at this age, it means confining the dog night and day, never giving him any freedom until you're absolutely sure he's housebroken. This can get to be a traumatic experience for both parties.

Make this a routine: feeding, finding out what his "schedule" is, and then going outside.

If you walk him give him a long leash — some dogs are shy.

Don't jerk him to encourage him on.

Have patience. Urge him on in an easy tone of voice.

Take him back to the same place he went before.

Romp with him for a few minutes after he does his business. Show him you're pleased.

A dog won't resent punishment if caught in the act.

A country dog that is grown and not curb-trained can present a problem if you must take him to the city for any length of time. A glycerine suppository can be used to get things started.

KINDERGARTEN PLAY LESSONS

It'll take about a week for the pup to settle into the new house, then you can start the simple play lessons. They're just what we say they are — play lessons. That means plenty of reward and no discipline, no matter what happens. It's not only a matter of what he learns; it's also a matter of liking the idea of school. But I've never seen a puppy yet that didn't learn all his ABC's on a leash by the time he was ready for real lessons at the age of twelve weeks.

What can you expect to teach between seven and twelve weeks? To walk fairly well at HEEL, and to know the commands SIT, STAY, and COME. He'll have learned that the leash means control; he'll have to do the things expected of him — when it's on he can't get away. It'll all be rather confusing to him at first, but when you put the leash on and give him commands he'll be getting plenty of love and attention, and that's good, and he'll like it.

And he'll be learning a lot of things on an unconscious level. These subtleties are among the means of learning. And they're the really important things he has to learn at this age. We're interested most in his attitude. It's better that he be happy and show a desire to please than do everything you want reluctantly.

It's just as important at this time to be handling the child correctly, too. This, of course, will depend much on the kid's age. You'll have to spell everything out in detail when working with a child as young as Gretchen. During the play periods the youngster has to be taught not to be too rough on a young pup. During the play lessons, just because the child wants the dog to do a certain thing doesn't mean that the puppy will respond or ought to. There should definitely be an understanding that the child doesn't go off by himself to train at any time. A child's attention span is longer than a puppy's. A child cannot recognize when the puppy has had enough. One of the reasons we want an adult in the picture is that the child should also be watched to see when he has had enough.

First we taught Gretchen how to hold the six-foot training leash. The right hand holds the neatly folded excess. The left is the important hand; with it the trainer controls the dog.

Obviously neither end of the leash knew what was meant by control. It's only natural, the pup will balk. A gentle nudge of the leash may bring him along. Gretchen had her own ideas.

FIRST WE LEARN TO CRAWL — THEN WALK

The pup can be walked on a leash about the ninth week. He'll have gotten used to the collar by this time. Impress upon the child that the leash is for control, not for dragging the dog.

It's customary to teach a dog to walk and stay at heel on the trainer's left side. The custom got started with hunting dogs. A right-handed hunter carries his gun on his right side; for safety's sake the dog was trained to stay on his left. But the same principle applies to the trainer carrying packages. A southpaw should train the dog for the right side.

In the next four pages we document exactly how both dog and child learned to handle the leash . . . one of them on either end.

She said she had better show him she still loved him. So, she then proceeded to plant a big kiss on his black snout. She started it all over and very much to my surprise . . .

. . . Tar got up and walked just as nice as you please. Dog was leading trainer, he was on the wrong side and walked where he wanted to. But, all these things didn't matter. The important thing was that they were walking. When we turn the page we'll show how we got them both straightened out. Note here the training collar on Tar. It's a choke collar made of chain. It's not for choking the dog but it does tighten when he exerts too much pressure on it. The trainer can release it by putting slack in the leash. The dog will learn to release it by not pulling. A sharp yank and the dog will soon learn the collar means control. This collar should be just big enough to slip over his head without too much slack. The dog shouldn't wear the chain collar when he runs free. The end ring could catch onto something and he would not be able to get himself free.

Something has interested him more than walking. With that much leash between Gretchen and Tar, control's lost. If she had him on a short leash, she could hold his head up to walk.

FIRST WE LEARN TO CRAWL — THEN WALK [continued]

We start all over. We now explain to Gretchen that the left hand and a short leash will be her control. She can hold the dog in any . . .

. . . position. With his head up he can't stop to sniff. He won't be able to get too far out in front or lag behind. He won't tangle . . .

. . . up in her legs. This is the end of the first session and already the two of them are walking together. This should not be a long lesson, no more than two attempts. If he won't do it wait and try next day. I've seen so many people drag a puppy along. It's wrong.

DROP THE DISHES AND SIT...ON COMMAND

The puppy can be started on command SIT just as soon as he has gotten the idea of how to walk on a leash. Hold the leash short, keep his head up. Just before the command SIT is given, the trainer should transfer the leash from his left hand to his right hand. Now the right hand is holding the dog's head up. Command SIT. Stop walking. The right hand pulls the dog's head up and back; at the same time the left hand pushes the dog's hindquarters down to the ground.

During these play lessons a puppy will learn this command in very short order. Within two days you'll see that the left hand doesn't have to exert much pressure at all. The dog will be sitting by the voice command, not the hand pressure. This is a good example of the way he learns by association. The hand explains to him what the word means. Remember, only use one word in the command . . . SIT. Discussion and argument interfere with his learning by word association.

Tar's now not quite ten weeks old. The secret is to teach the commands on a training leash. Gretchen, showing more confidence in even this short time, has all the control. Tar cannot run off.

SIT, STAY, COME, BE HAPPY

Now we build from one learned thing to the next. This was the first time Gretchen and Tar tried these commands. Look how successful they were.

We've learned SIT. Hold him in place with the leash, walk in front of him so he sees you. Repeat SIT, use the finger to emphasize the command. Command STAY. Show him the signal the traffic cop uses. There isn't much else he can do on a tight leash. Take a step back and release the leash. Command STAY. He most likely did it because Gretchen looked so awkward...

... Take another step back giving the signal and repeating the command. He won't be able to hold very long. Watch, if you see he is going to break be ready to command COME . . .

. . . Gretchen got to the full six feet of the leash before Tar started to lose interest and look away. I told her to quickly have him come. Be ready to anticipate what the dog is going to do. It's much better to have a puppy do something right when he's ready . . .

. . . than do it wrong. Gretchen was briefed ahead of time to get on her knee to give command COME. Kneeling for this command is important. He'll come quicker if he sees you're friendly . . .

. . . The leash is still the control. If he doesn't know what you mean by COME give a little tug on the leash. Bring him into you hand over hand. All three of us were so very pleased.

NO, NO, THE COMMAND IS NO

These kindergarten lessons are still play games. We don't reprimand for "sleeping in class" . . . yet. We try to do everything on the reward side of the report card. But NO is just as much of a command as SIT or STAY. When you say NO . . . mean it. One of the ways to end up with an unruly dog — or, for that matter, an unruly child — is to say NO and have no follow-through. Let's have no nonsense about this; accept no compromise here.

THE COMMAND IS NO — FOR YOU, TOO

Sugar and spice? Yes, but that's not all . . . part devil. It's very important that the child doesn't take advantage of the teaching situation. Kids can get a lot of satisfaction out of playing the role of teacher. But if not watched they may really put too many demands on their pupil. Gretchen is being reprimanded here by Mother because she was making Tar fetch over and over and over again in the broiling hot sun. They had both learned this new trick. Tar wanted to stop and get in the shade, but Gretchen wanted more.

GRADUATING FROM KINDERGARTEN

Some dogs grow up not liking: strange people, strange dogs, strange noises, riding in cars, walking in town, and a host of other things. By this time our puppy is really part of our family because we put him into all kinds of situations at an early age . . . like going downtown. He accepts it as part of life and it's a good place to test all he's learned in preschool.

Some days you can't make a buck. Somebody... ... forgot their lessons. Gretchen works it ...

... out herself. She gets pup's collar fixed ... ... Then she has to get the leash rolled up ...

65

... Off they go again only to meet another ... ... problem. But if you don't get too excited when strange dogs come around, your dog won't get upset. People have a tendency to yank their dogs away. Dogs like to make friends.

THAT WAS KINDERGARTEN

As we look back over our progress so far, what was the most important phase of the preschool period? There's no question about it — the play games and the socializing between the trainer and the puppy were the most important. What we've tried to do is to give the puppy a specific personality and a strong desire to learn. We've controlled the environment to produce this. We've irritated him to teach him tolerance. We've cared for him to make him feel secure. We've taught him some lessons to develop a sense of responsibility. We've spent a lot of time playing with him just to show him that we love him. . . . What more could a mother do?

The way you live and the specific situation with your dog may not be the same as Gretchen and Tar's. We've tried to illustrate the philosophy of handling a dog in this period. These critical five weeks are basically the new principle in our training. If you understand the principle there's no reason why you can't change and interpret this to fit your specific circumstances. For example, these pictures would have been a lot different if Gretchen lived in an apartment.

Chapter 5

The Dog Goes To School

We've spent five weeks in kindergarten preparing the puppy for this next phase, going to school. One of the most interesting findings of the research at Hamilton Station in Maine concerned the necessity for the continuation without interruption of the training at this specific time, the twelfth week. It's important to recognize that the next four to six weeks are the most important training time in the dog's life. I know it's hard to believe, but this scientific study (see page 14) means that a dog when twelve weeks old must be carefully trained to get the best out of him in the future. Prior to this study, most trainers considered a twelve-week pup as an infant. Of course they didn't know that the brain of the pup at this age has attained full adult form and that he's already in the last phase of his mental development. He's ready to learn. He's ready for work. The play lessons have ended.

In the next few weeks he'll try you for size to see if you have the nerve to reprimand him. We're going to teach him the basic commands and now they'll be taught on a conscious level of learning, which only means that the dog will know darn right well that he's being taught.

In four hours or so of class lessons — that is, about three to four weeks of ten-minutes-a-day lessons — your pup will have put finishing touches on commands SIT, STAY, COME, HEEL, KENNEL, and some manners that will make it possible for you all to live together — each in his own place. In the play lessons we used the leash for control and as a means of actually doing the commands. For example, when we taught COME, the leash was used to bring him in to you if he didn't understand what was meant by the command. Now he'll be taught almost all commands without the leash; he'll respond to the voice or signal. The leash will be used only if he gets balky; then we'll attach it and *make* him go through the commands, just like a baby in kindergarten.

There's a trick that often works with a puppy that knows his lessons but gets bored. Change the classroom. If you've been training in the back yard, take him to a park; he'll get peppy.

67

Tar is twelve weeks old. He has learned his lessons on the leash. He's started to respond to the voice commands. Note that just the touching of his hind quarters reminds him command SIT means SIT. They're ready to start school. See (right) what a sense of accomplishment and rapport does for teacher and pupil.

Start this command as before, he's walking at heel. Command SIT. Take a step forward to ...

... show him the new hand signal, a downward motion of the finger. Make sure he sees it.

Within the next week or so spring the voice and hand commands on him when he's not expecting them. If he doesn't respond, quietly go to him, repeat the commands, and make him sit. If he has moved away before you get to him take him back to where he was when the command was given. Don't scold him. Within another week he'll respond to either of the signals.

SIT ... BY VOICE, BY SIGNAL

The dog will learn by association and repetition. And it's no extra effort for you or the dog to have him learn his commands not only by voice or whistle, but by hand signals as well. All three are taught at the same time. The pictures won't show Gretchen using a whistle. For a child this young, we figured that she had enough to learn teaching voice and hand signals.

Here's how all three work. The voice command is given simultaneously with the hand signal for that command, and immediately afterward — if desired — the whistle signal (example: one blast for SIT) is given. By this time the dog knows the voice command from preschool where it was taught by pushing him into a sitting position. Now he sees and hears another signal when he's supposed to sit. By repeating these three signals together, he'll associate the new ones — the dropped extended finger or the one whistle blast — with the one he already knows — the voice command. Within a week he'll do the command on any one of the signals.

BRICK BY BRICK WE BUILD — SIT...STAY...COME

We go back and reinforce what we've already learned and build from there. You can see that even Gretchen isn't as awkward as she was when she tried this in kindergarten. We increase the dog's vocabulary, command by command: SIT is first, STAY is next, then COME is a natural. The command COME is taught a number of ways. If you see that the puppy isn't responding well enough, instead of doing it as Gretchen shows in the pictures, try a second method. When you have the puppy sitting in the STAY position, clap your hands, make a big commotion, turn away, and run from the dog and call COME . . . COME. He'll come . . . to play.

Tar's thirteen weeks old. Without the leash he is told to sit. As he's shown the hand signal for stay, the voice command is firmly repeated STAY. STAY. The traffic cop sign is . . .

. . . extended toward him as you slowly step back. Don't move fast or jerkily, he'll break . . .

71

... and come to you. If he does, start it over. Try to work back, don't let him wait long ...

... Bend down, command COME in a friendly tone. Show him you want to be friends; he does!

Gretchen's not allowed to spank Tar; she's too young. But when he gets obstreperous she has to show him who's the boss. She's allowed to take him roughly by the collar and lead him back to where he started to show off and settle him down, then start the lesson over. Teach him who gives the command in this game.

At this age the dog is going to express his independence just like a kid in the fourth grade. He's going to try himself to see what he can do and try you to see what he can get away with. You can almost see this happen with a pup. With Tar it happened when he was sixteen weeks old. One of Tar's litter-mates that was trained by an adult under this accelerated system expressed her independence during the seventeenth week. The exact time will vary, but the way they express their independence is the same: they act as though they never heard the command before . . . they get preoccupied with a very important smell . . . they get very tired and just have to lie down . . . they walk away and refuse to obey the command. When this happens, a firm hand must be used; it will most likely mean a spanking. This will teach the dog that you mean business; if he learns it now, this could be the only spanking you'll ever have to give the dog. From now on a threatening gesture on the part of the trainer will be enough.

There should be an understanding with a trainer who's under teen age that he won't be allowed to punish the pup by spanking. But a trainer must be able to use reprimand. When it becomes obvious that the puppy is out to prove that he's going to be the boss, the adult should take over the training for a few days. See to it that the dog receives the necessary discipline and then get things back to an even keel.

A threatening gesture can get things back on an even keel. Gretchen's show of displeasure will hurt him just as much as a good spanking.

Command SIT, STAY firmly. Show the signal. ... command over your shoulder, give the sign
Then start to slowly walk away. Repeat the ... to stay behind you as you walk out of his ...

STAY A WHILE — HAVE A SEAT

This finishing touch can be very useful. There are many occasions when you want to keep your dog out of the way while you have a chore to do. He has to learn to sit and stay until released, even if you're out of sight. I've known this command to save a dog's life, but the main purpose is to teach the dog good manners; the SIT, STAY command can keep the dog out of some youngster's ice cream cone at the drugstore.

You should start using this method of extending the STAY command at about fourteen weeks of age. Don't overdo; remember a pup has a very short attention span. It's not the length of time at first; it's his waiting until released that's important.

75

... sight. First time only for a few seconds, ... Command STAY. Gradually increase the
then be ready to come back into his view ... time you leave the yard. Fool him after a bit...

... Walk all around the house. Let'm guess
where and when you'll return. Try to fool him.

HEEL ... DO IT, DON'T BE ONE

The command HEEL always brings to mind the story of the new dog owner who brought his Great Dane puppy to obedience class the first time with the back of his left shoe torn out. The cut line for the story is, "He's learning his commands by taste."

Having your dog at your side while walking down the street is desirable for obvious reasons — he's out of your way and out of the way of others. A real pain in the neck is the mutt that only wants to be the leader of the band — out front. A dog shouldn't be walking you. But you won't have this problem if you start him in preschool to walk on leash. The choke collar soon teaches him his place if he insists on being a puller. There's no use rushing to teach him to walk at heel off the leash; it's hard to keep a growing pup under such control. If you walk him on leash short enough he'll automatically learn his place.

As soon as he starts to walk on a leash he should learn to walk on his own feet. Shove him gently out of your way with your leg ...

... Be sure to supervise the child; don't let them kick the dog. Explain that the handler's hand pressure will keep him in his place.

If he grows up to be a puller use the choke collar and a stout stick to hold him back . . .

. . . Keep tapping him with the stick. If he does not want to get the idea give him a swat with it. Very soon the stick will only be needed as a reminder. Every time you pull the choke or tap him command HEEL. When he has the idea release the choke collar. Give some praise . . .

. . . Without the stick, hold the leash in the right hand and slap your leg with the left. This will be his signal to heel up. Next, if he decides to change his pace or stop to smell give him a yank, slap at your leg, and command HEEL. Then when you think he has learned this change your pace, walk in circles. Teach him that he's walking with you, not you with him.

78

LEARNING TO CROSS THE STREET

The two biggest dog killers are distemper and automobiles. Keep your dog out of the street. The first day puppy goes to school he learns to cross the street. This is a safety measure. We never, but never, cross over, even if the way is clear, without first giving the SIT command. Then, off we walk on command HEEL. I'm not saying that left to his own devices a dog will come to a curb, SIT, look up and down the street, then cross. But it will teach him to slow up and not bolt out into traffic. If you never cross without going through this ritual he'll learn by the time he's a young adult to wait for you as a child will do. He learns this on the unconscious level of learning — a curb means stop because that's what he's always done.

Command SIT in front of the kennel. The command was SIT but I guess that'll have to do for a pup eleven weeks old. Point to the door and command KENNEL. Keep giving the command, start moving him with gentle force. Point and command, point and command, then shove.

KENNEL UP — OUTSIDE

If you have an outside run for your dog, it's going to be to your advantage to be able to command the dog to go into the kennel. You'll appreciate this little refinement on rainy days when you won't want to go out with him. This is a very easy command to teach. As you can see, Tar learned it in two simple lessons.

The second lesson went so easily that Gretchen decided to find out just how much fun it was.

KENNEL...................................... ... COME ....

...Now all together........................ ... It's fun ....

83

...Fooled!

KENNEL UP — INSIDE

The Kennel-Aire cage makes an excellent means of traveling with a dog. The cage folds down flat, is very light and easy to handle. We keep one set up inside for a pup for two reasons. The first, so he'll get used to it and learn to like it, since he may have to live in it for many hours when traveling by car. The second reason is the exact opposite of what these pictures show. A dog should have some place around the house where he can have some peace and quiet. It was a good idea at first to have Gretchen show Tar that this was fun. We soon had to tell her to leave him alone when he went into his kennel.

KENNEL UP — LET'S TRAVEL

Now that you have the pup used to the cage, you're ready to take him to some parties. Well, that is you go to the parties and puppy stays locked in the Kennel-Aire in the car. At first he'll try to raise the roof, but in the cage he can't do any damage to the car or to himself. Let him bark himself to sleep. He'll get the idea sooner or later that this is where he's to live when we all go traveling in the car. Don't try this with him while the car is parked at your home — he won't understand. Don't go to the car to hush him — that's what he wants. He'll think that barking makes you come and he'll sing loud.

The Kennel-Aire makes a fine place for Towser to live while on the road. He can see everything that goes on without being in everybody's hair and smearing up the windows. It's good for the driver, too — he can see through the cage for rear-view vision.

Traveling with a pooch is nothing new. The Vikings took dogs to Nova Scotia, the Romans took them to Gaul, Columbus to America, and Miles Standish took one to Priscilla. At first have plenty of papers around — a young pup may get motion sickness. If you're going on a long trip, wait to feed him when you arrive. Don't give him any water for an hour or two before the jaunt. Be sure that he gets plenty of air while riding and that he can sit up to see what's going on; this will help to prevent motion sickness. But if he starts to drool, he's getting nervous. Stop and let him walk around a bit. It's always good to get a young pup started with short trips, and if need be, for long trips you can use tranquilizers. If the dog seems frightened, try feeding him in the car while you have it parked in your driveway. Let him associate something good with the noisy jalopy. He may get to love the motion so much that he'll want to hang his head out the window and play like he's on a fire engine.

This sight-seer who hangs his head out the window, sneering at the passing cars and all the dogs that have to walk, causes all kinds of discomfort for people passengers. Towser wants the window seat and the window down, even in winter. Don't encourage this, not only for your own comfort, but it's very bad for the dog's eyes and ears.

Just as bad as the sight-seer is the traveling lap dog who assumes the affectionate, devoted position in the driver's lap. He remains still while the car is in motion but stands up and gets hair in the driver's mouth when he takes it upon himself to see what's causing the stalled traffic ahead.

85

As a tiny pup lift him onto the tailgate, command KENNEL, then let him walk in. When he's big enough to jump he'll know what you want. The cage makes a perfect house. When we set up camp the first thing we do is make up the doghouse to get him out of the way. At night he sleeps here. He generates enough body heat so that he'll be snug. The cover holds in heat.

Absolutely never let this get started. Firmly command NO. If need be give him a shove. One slip on this and he'll continue to beg, hoping that eventually you'll renege again. Don't let any guests be "kind" to your dog and slip him a tidbit. He'll finally come to realize that the table is not the place where he gets fed. He should have his own dishes, his own place to eat.

MANNERS MAKE THE MAN
...AND THE DOG

SIT, STAY. It's a good time to brush up on . . .

As man developed through the centuries, he supposedly began to live more by manners than by animal instincts. We don't tolerate ill-mannered people and the same thing should apply to dogs. A mean dog is ill-mannered. Some dogs have a tendency toward a vicious temperament through heredity. We feel that these don't make good family pets, but a puppy can develop a mean streak by being teased in puppyhood. A puppy that has a tantrum and growls and snaps with rage isn't funny. People often tease puppies to bring on this rage, thinking it's cute. This can only lead to trouble. Don't grab bones or toys away from the puppy, and don't let anyone disturb him while he's eating. It's only natural that he'll want to protect what's rightly his. Tug of wars are bad because they teach a dog the power of his teeth and jaws.

. . . lessons. He should wait like a gentleman.

Table manners are an indication of culture and fine breeding. Just tell that to a puppy as you go to hand him a bone. He'll grab it out of instinct. Don't pull it back away from him — that'll only teach him to grab and pull. Just hold on to it and make sure that he doesn't get it until you speak harshly to him and if necessary give him a light whack across the nose. This might surprise him. If he lets go and then comes back and takes the bone gently, let him have it.

It's only natural, he'll join you on the . . . . . . soft couch. Command NO. If he doesn't . . .

. . . get your point lift him off by his paws. Command NO. Spank him if you enter a room . . .

. . . find him on a chair. Also test him, see if he just got down. Is a cushion still warm?

Puppies go through a stage where they destroy things. It usually happens when they're cutting teeth or when they're just bored. Be sure pup has some bones and toys around to chew on. Also take a few minutes to play with him. This will take care of his boredom. As far as his teething, you're just going to have to watch him through this period. More about it on page 141. Remember, your guests may not like a pup's sharp teeth. Reprimand him with a sharp NO when he starts to chew on clothing. He will not be able to distinguish between a cotton house dress and a satin Cassini gown.

PARLOR MANNERS

Never let bad habits get started and corrections won't have to be made. If your dog decides to sneak onto the furniture when you're out of the room and this act is verboten, the best way to cure him is to set a couple of mousetraps on the cushions. When he jumps up onto the furniture, they'll go off and he'll have nobody to blame but himself. Just remember that if you allow your dog to sit on the furniture at home with his muddy paws and with the problems of shedding, he'll most likely do the same when he's visiting. Of course a dog should have his own place to lie down — a blanket or a pad of some kind.

90

SHOW YOUR MANNERS TO FRIENDS ON THE STREET

There's nothing so impolite as a dog who jumps on your friends. Those dogs that feel they have to dominate the conversation and hold all the attention are just spoiled brats. It's easy enough to control this situation. Just tell the dog to SIT and STAY. Do this every time the situation arises. While you're training the puppy to be minding his own business, ask your friends not to make a fuss over him and pat him. Later when he learns his place he can be patted by·the stranger and he'll still keep his place.

To keep a pup down, push his nose back down with the palm of your hand. With a grown dog take him by the paws, bring up a knee, throw him off backwards, give a sharp NO command.

DOWN

Unfortunately, when a dog jumps up he's trying to show you that he likes you and that he wants to be friends. But he's not paying the cleaning bills. To teach the puppy DOWN, pressing the palm of your hand against the dog's nose will often do the trick. Some trainers suggest stepping on the dog's hind feet when he jumps up. I don't like this. A shoe can damage a paw. The best way to handle his jumping is with a knee from underneath. It will be quite a surprise since he is expecting a pat. Since he can't see the knee coming and won't know where the blow came from he'll quickly learn that this is not a desired position to be in because he usually ends up on the flat of his back. A dog may learn not to jump on the person who has trained him but he may continue to jump on friends or strangers. This can be a rather frightening experience. Get a few friends to cooperate and give him the same treatment when he jumps up on them. He'll soon learn that DOWN means the same thing for everybody.

Chapter 6

Game Time... Let's Do Some Tricks

Once the dog becomes a good citizen and has learned his lessons, you can try him on some games. This is much fun for the trainer and the dog. Since your dog has been trained to learn to learn, you're going to be surprised how fast he catches on to doing tricks.

LET'S SHAKE HANDS

The most common trick is to shake hands. It's rather easy to teach. Command the dog to SIT, STAY. Of course then the trainer is to SIT, STAY facing the dog. Tap the under side of the dog's paw. He'll take his weight off that leg. Command SHAKE HANDS, lift the paw, praise him. Try it a number of times each day. He'll get it fast. If not, try this: if you're shaking hands with the right hand, hold him by the collar under the throat with the left hand. As you command SHAKE HANDS and tap him on the under side of the leg, throw his weight to his left to take the weight off the right paw. Then you pick it up. Now he'll get the idea. He may even get elected mayor.

LET'S TALK IT OVER

Noisy dogs learn the command SPEAK with ease. When they bark, command SPEAK. Praise them. If the dog needs a little incentive, try this at mealtime. Let him smell the food, get him excited, and command SPEAK. An excited tone of voice will get him going.

The quiet dog is the one that's a little harder to teach. It'll take a little more patience; you'll have to wait until he uses his voice, then be ready with the command SPEAK. Be sure the tone of your voice is friendly. You don't want him to think he should stop, even though he's barking at a stranger.

Take advantage of any part of the dog's routine to put across the meaning. For example, if he's in the habit of going for a walk at a certain time, take the leash to the door, get him excited. Talk to him; don't open the door until he makes a noise. Command SPEAK and praise him.

I know one dog that wouldn't bark but she cried every time anyone left the house — like all good poodles she wanted to go, too. The whimpering was very easily turned into a bark on the command SPEAK by encouraging the dog to use her voice. Your dog is now well on the way to becoming a disc jockey.

FETCH ... TEACHING HIM HOW

1. Using a feather, or a soft toy, get the dog excited. Jump around, make him really want...

3. Throw it a few feet. Point, command FETCH.

2 . . . to catch it. Let him chase you, prance around. It is fun! Now he's just about ready.

4. He will, but how do we make him deliver it?

5. Gretchen called but he had his own ideas. Then she made the mistake of running after him. He thought it was his turn to get her all excited. The trick to make him come is for Gretchen to run away from him commanding COME in an excited tone of voice. If he drops it, go to the object, point and say FETCH. He will after a few false starts. There is a good lesson in these pictures, a perfect example of what not to do. Never bolt at a dog.

FETCH ... THE FINISHING TOUCH ON ALL COMMANDS

1. Command SIT..........................

2 ... Command STAY........................

3 ... Then show............................

4 ...Then throw...............................

97

5 . . . Then go, command FETCH . . . .

6 . . . Get down on his level. As a last resort if you can't get him to come in, put him on a long leash and bring him in hand over hand.

7. The key: always the same, plenty of praise.

FETCH ... FOR FUN IN WATER

All dogs are born with the knowledge of how to swim. A dog'll do it if he has to, but unless he's grown up around water he may need a little coaxing to get him started. One way of getting him in is to go in yourself. Then call him in, make it look like fun. The other way is to take a stick or any other object that will float and toss it in shallow water so that he can get it only by wading. Command FETCH. Gradually work him in deeper. After his first stroke he'll swim; he'll love this.

Gretchen throws a small boat bumper out in the water after she has commanded Tar to SIT and STAY. Then she points to it and tells him to FETCH. He'll swim out now that he knows how. Urge him home with plenty of loud praise.

Tar was 24 weeks old when these pictures were taken. See how in a short time we taught this.

LIE DOWN

For a puppy or a work dog, command SIT is given either to get him out of the way if necessary or to exercise the control over him that's needed in training. Many trainers consider LIE DOWN a command; we don't. There are no useful commands that get taught from the prone position, only tricks. So for our purposes LIE DOWN is taught as a trick.

The conventional method of teaching LIE DOWN is with the leash put under the trainer's foot. The dog is pulled into the LIE DOWN position. This method should be your last resort because he will only resent this sort of treatment, and he should. Before he even knows what's expected of him he's being shoved and pushed. It's too confusing.

The first thing to do is to put him in the SIT, STAY position. Show him the hand signal — palm up, hand held above the head, then slowly move the hand swinging it down toward the ground. Repeat LIE DOWN, LIE DOWN. Some dogs learn what is wanted just by this hand signal and voice. Turn the page and you'll see two methods of teaching LIE DOWN.

If he doesn't understand the hand and voice signal for lie down, have him sit. Command LIE DOWN. Take hold of his paws, lift them and all the while keep repeating LIE DOWN. Pull . . .

LIE DOWN BY TWO METHODS

Before using the conventional method as shown below, try the method above, since pulling the dog down by the leash can get him excited. If he becomes frantic he might thrash around and learn to hate doing this — and rightly so.

With the stubborn dog it's often a useful thing to show him that you can make him do it by using the method shown below. Then go back again and try the method above.

With the dog that creeps toward you on his belly, the pulling of the

Attach the leash to the choke collar, run the leash under your foot. Show him the hand . . . . . . signal and then command LIE DOWN. If he thinks you're just waving at him give . . .

... him out toward you. Then put the extended paws on the ground. To make sure he understands what is meant by this, put pressure on his shoulders. Hold him down, give him praise.

leash method will soon cure him. It's important here to make it fun for him
to respond to this.

Keep the tone of voice very quiet when the dog is finally in the LIE
DOWN position. If you praise him with too much excitement he'll want to
jump up to accept your praise.

Some dogs roll over on their backs when they're doing this training.
This usually means that the dog is frightened. When this happens, give the
dog plenty of praise, but immediately get him up into the sitting position
and then start over again. Repeat this until the dog no longer rolls over.

... a tug on the leash. Then let up. If he still ... his head right to the ground. Lean over,
won't go down start over but this time pull ... force him all the way down. Now speak gently.

PLAY POSSUM

Teaching the dog to play possum is started in the SIT, STAY position. The first thing the trainer must do is give the signal of the dropped hand for LIE DOWN. The trainer is then pointing at the floor. The verbal command PLAY DEAD or PLAY POSSUM should then be given. When the dog lies down the trainer should then roll him on his side, repeat the command a number of times, very gently stroking the dog and holding his head down. He'll have a tendency to lift his head. Every time he goes to raise it, put a little pressure on him and quietly tell him PLAY DEAD. As you can see, this is a fun game for both Tar and Gretchen.

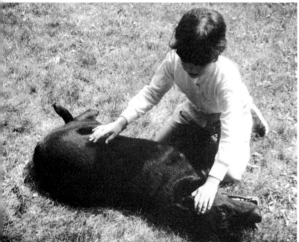

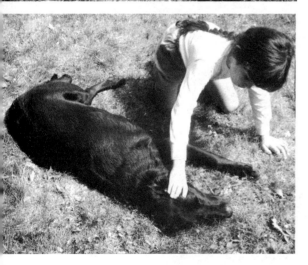

Tar is only a little over four months old and Gretchen's so pleased, he learned it so fast.

105

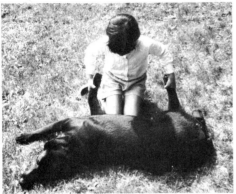

ROLL OVER

The dog is put in the SIT, STAY position, then told to LIE DOWN. He's rolled over on his side. Take his two underneath legs and slightly lift them so that he starts to roll over on his back. When he's all the way over, let go. The command is ROLL OVER, ROLL OVER. Repeat this a few times. After you flip him over, he'll most likely jump to his feet. Make sure that you give him plenty of praise. It's necessary that the dog realize that there are two separate commands here. The first one is LIE DOWN with its signal. The hand signal for ROLL OVER will be a circular motion of the hand.

Roll over should be taught after playing dead.

No kissing on the dance floor please. She's trying some intricate steps, Tar's Twisting.

SOME BALLROOM MANEUVERS

All little girls like to dance. It's not always the same for dogs. Small dogs can usually stand on their hind legs with much more ease than the larger breeds. Young puppies have a difficult time sitting and begging or dancing since their back muscles haven't developed. As much as Gretchen tried, she just couldn't make Tar stand on his back legs. He was just too heavy. He wouldn't even do it for food. So she concocted her own dancing lessons and she was the partner.

The way to teach a dog to dance on his back legs is to hold some food above his head. When he stands on his back legs to reach the food he dances. Move your hand in a circle so that he'll have to move around and he'll soon learn to follow the hand; he'll learn to turn. Be sure that you always give him this little tidbit for all his work.

108

Tar and Gretchen had a job while on vacation. Every day they walked to the mailbox to get the newspaper. They both loved this chore.

LET'S CARRY OUR SHARE

There's nothing that gives a dog more pleasure than some useful work. Carrying the mail, the newspaper, or a package from the market is a lot of fun for both dog and trainer.

We've already taught him how to FETCH. Command HOLD should be taught while he's on a leash. Take an object such as a rolled-up newspaper, put it on the ground in front of him, command him to FETCH. As soon as he has taken it into his mouth command HOLD. If he drops the object, repeat the FETCH command. When he picks the object up the second time, put your hand around his muzzle and command HOLD. Walk him with the object in his mouth. If he drops the object as he starts to walk, start all over again. If he doesn't get the idea and has a desire to keep dropping the object, try scratching him on the ears while he has his mouth full. This'll take his mind off the desire to drop the article. Try to anticipate when he's going to drop, tap him under the chin, and command HOLD, HOLD. He'll catch on rapidly.

Avoid training the command HOLD in extremely hot weather. A dog perspires by panting. He won't grip an object firmly if he must hold his mouth open in order to breathe.

109

NOW LET'S DROP IT

Never pull an object out of a dog's mouth. You can hurt his teeth and you can teach him that his jaws are very strong. The command DROP is a very easy one to teach. With the object held in his mouth the dog is told to SIT. The trainer then flicks the finger, striking his nose. The command is given and the flick is repeated until he finally drops the object.

Tar hates to have his nose flicked by a finger so he learned DROP fast. Notice that the object Tar carries is a brush. He learns to hold an object very gingerly or his mouth will get pricked. Brush teaches soft mouth.

Tar's not very happy about this. But that's learning! Sometimes it's just a dog's life.

LET'S STAND UP

There are a number of ways of teaching a dog to stand. Put the dog in the SIT, STAY position, then command STAND. Put your hands firmly under his belly, lift his hindquarters, and command STAND. Pat him gently and give him praise. If he goes to sit down, just tap him a few times under the belly. Repeat the command. If he starts to creep toward you, give him a sharp rap across the nose and tell him to STAND. Once again give him praise.

Some dogs will respond to this command when their backs are scratched. They seem to stand and want more. Neither of these systems worked with Tar. He was too heavy for Gretchen to lift so a loop was made in the leash and she held him up in position. When he would go to sit down she would hold him up and give the command STAND. In no time at all she could release the leash, have him stand, and walk around in front of him. All the time she was releasing the leash and walking around in front of him she was quietly telling him to STAND.

It's surprising to realize that a dog learns these games in a matter of minutes.

111

OTHER GAMES

Beg . . . Under certain conditions your dog is going to be allowed to beg — not when he wants but when you want. Put him on the leash. Tell him to SIT and STAY. Hold a piece of meat above his head. As he starts to get up off his front feet command BEG, but don't give him the food until he is actually sitting up. If he comes up on his back legs and tries to stand in order to get it, take the food away. Put him back in the SIT position and start all over again. The hand that leads the leash can help guide him up, but don't put too much pressure on his collar. Give him plenty of encouragement. Another way of teaching BEG is to put the dog in the SIT, STAY position, take his front paws and sit him up in a sitting position, and give the voice command BEG. Try to help him learn how to balance himself.

Saying Prayers . . . Put the puppy in the SIT, STAY position in front of a bench or the bed. Place his front paws up on the bed, command PRAYERS. Gently push his head down. At the same time, put a little tidbit of food between his eyes. Release him by saying OK. Keep repeating this until he gets the idea that he's to put his head down.

Nose Balancer . . . To teach him to balance something on his nose put him in the SIT, STAY position. Take a small piece of dog biscuit, place it between his eyes, and tell him to wait. Release him by saying OK. He may soon learn to flip it off his nose and catch it. This will take a lot of practice but he'll like doing this because it means something to eat.

112

Chapter 7

Growing Pains

We mentioned earlier that the dog's brain reaches full physical maturity at a very young age; as he matures in experience he'll pick up bad habits along with the good and he'll necessarily need some correction. No matter how well we train him as a pup, he'll have to be shown what's expected of him as he encounters new situations. You can't tell these things to a dog; you have to show them.

We feel that our method of early training, when followed to the letter, will produce a puppy that you'll be able to guide along as he encounters his new situations. Major corrections will not be necessary. The simple training tools which we have shown you will be adequate. Your dog has been conditioned favorably to respond to your expressions of pleasure and displeasure. The important thing is not so much the specific problem as it is the timely application of the correct solution. For example, a friend of ours had a problem of his dog stealing food. He corrected it by a method we will show you in this section — tin cans tied on a string. His dog developed another problem, "lifting his leg" in the garage. He came to me for a method of correcting this. I suggested the same trick — tin cans tied on a string. He was surprised that the same corrective method was to be tried in both cases. A good teacher or trainer has to be able to adapt, improvise, and use his imagination with the training tools at his disposal.

The three "tools" to be used on the six-month young adult dog are: the Long Rope, the Assistant, the Tin Cans.

THE LONG ROPE... can be used on the dog that bolts or runs from the trainer. This is annoying if the dog bolts from the house or the yard, but it can be particularly dangerous when the dog bolts from a car. Some dogs will play a game with you and bolt on call. They know better; they're just trying you. In all these cases the correction is much the same. But unless the dog is a small one I don't recommend that a young trainer try this. Of course, a teenager can manage, but in all cases gloves must — repeat, must — be worn.

Suppose you take your dog for a run in the park. You take him off the leash and say, "Go on, Towser, have yourself a good run." The next thing you know he's two blocks away. Next time take a long rope with you — fifty feet will do. Nylon is best; it's light and will slip around bushes or trees. Tie this rope to his choke collar, unhook his leash, put on your gloves to prevent rope burn, let him run. He'll think he's free. When he bolts for destination unknown let him go. When he gets to the end of the rope, command COME and then yank. Jerk him tail over teacups. He'll get up and wonder what that was all about.

A few such episodes and he'll start to respect the command COME. Let him drag the rope around on these outings. If he decides to test his freedom, step on the rope, pick it up, let him have it.

The important thing is that the dog isn't going to know how long the rope is. When you think he has learned that you have this strange control over him at this distance you can take him off the long rope.

Many dogs become rope smart. They'll obey when they know the leash or rope is attached. As soon as they feel their freedom they'll try you. The long rope teaches them they don't have their freedom. So, after the long rope has established the dog's respect for the "long arm of the law," attach a short piece that will just drag behind him. The dog won't be able to estimate the difference in weight or drag. He isn't going to know how long the rope is. On a short rope you can fool him into thinking you have control over him. All he knows is that you have a line attached to his collar and he's learned that that spells trouble. The rope — long or short — will now be your long-distance control. There's a place in this training when the trainer's judgment is going to be all-important. You'll have to be sure when the dog has really learned not to bolt, because if you made the switch to the short rope before he was through trying you, you're going to be caught with your long rope down. Then you'll have to start all over. It usually takes about two weeks to cure a bolter. The important thing in this handling is not to rush things.

Professional dog handlers often use slingshots, air guns, and such to make corrections in their dogs at a distance. This is definitely *not* recommended for the amateur trainer. A professional will get the results desired quicker than you will, but the results won't necessarily be better. A pro knows how to use these tools. Safe distances, safe angle, and when they're needed come from the experience of handling many dogs. But I've never known a dog that needed this kind of treatment when started in his training at the correct age of seven weeks and handled properly.

We caught Tar stealing food. The tin cans ...

In many places it's against the law for dogs to bother livestock. Tar was an offender. Tin cans scared him out of this one in a hurry.

115

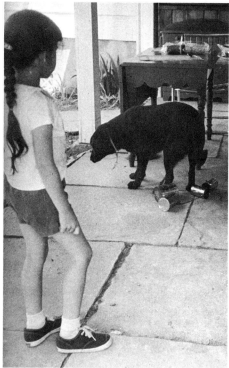

... straightened this out. We wanted more pictures; we never got them — he never stole again.

THE CAN THAT FEEDS HIM ALSO TRAINS HIM

Take four empty cans, punch holes in the side of each. String them together with stout cord. This is one of the best training devices ever invented. It can be useful to make all sorts of corrections. A loud clatter coming from behind will sure cure a dog of some bad habits in a hurry.

You may need an assistant to help with some of the problems you might run into. For example, if your dog gets into the neighbor's garbage can have the neighbor — if he's still speaking to you — help correct the dog. The four cans flung at him will discourage him and send him home with his tail between his legs.

I know of a case where the dog lived in an outside kennel. In the middle of the night he took to barking. The dog's owner, screaming QUIET from the second-story window, was making as much noise as the dog. So Master, who wanted a hunting dog, was sent out by wife into the cold each night to quiet Towser in order to protect her social position in the neighborhood. Towser cooperated, to the point that he would wait until Master was back in bed and warm again before he would start barking. Strategy was called for. A wire was strung between the second-story bedroom window and the dog kennel. Four cans were attached to a pulley. A number of such rigs were made and tied into place on the wire. The trainer lost sleep that night but he sure had fun. Every time the dog as much as let out a woof the string holding the pulley was cut. Down crashed the cans, making quite a clatter against the doghouse. The dog was scared into being quiet. With this repeated dive-bombing, it didn't take the dog long to learn that all hell broke loose when he barked, so he'd better shut up. The neighbors never did learn what the clatter in the middle of the night was. No one really cares now; the neighbors are happy — they're sleeping.

CHASING CARS ... can be corrected by using two assistants, the cans to produce three surprises. Use a car the dog doesn't know. You, the trainer, hide in the car so the dog can't see you. One assistant drives the car past your home and Towser, the neighborhood daredevil, charges. The other assistant hits him with the cans for surprise number one. Stop the car. Just to make sure that he's learned his lesson, you jump out of the car making a lot of noise. This will be the second surprise — he never expected to see you. Giving him a good licking — that's the third. Send him home, shaken but cured.

Some trainers are using an electronic collar for this kind of training. The trainer can give the dog a shock by radio. It won't hurt the dog but it'll make him stop what he's doing. This is another professional tool not for the amateur to fuss with.

The cans, to be successful in a training situation, must be used in such a way that the dog is surprised. He has to get the idea that what he's doing causes the clatter and racket. For example, if he has a habit of going into a closet, hang the cans so that when he paws the door open the cans will fall. These are simply lessons in cause and effect. And the effect will cause him to stop.

When Tar stole the food in the pictures on the preceding page, we deliberately put some food near the edge of the table. We took the pictures. As he stole the food the cans were thrown. Then we tried to have him do it again in order to get more pictures. He refused and has never tried to steal again. Which reminds me of the woman who was sitting crying in her kitchen when her husband came home from work. He asked her what was the matter. She blurted out that the dog had stolen a pie she had baked. The man sympathized and told her not to cry — he'd buy her a new dog.

Nor will he dig holes now or chase bicycles. Throwing the cans and hitting him won't hurt him, it'll surprise him and that's what we're after. He soon learns to associate the noise with all those things that are not allowed.

1. The "stranger" invites Tar into his car . . .

DON'T GET DOGNAPPED

A perfect example of where an assistant is needed in training. This person and his car should be completely strange to the dog. The dog should just happen to be alone when the "stranger" drives up in front of the house.

In certain areas of the country there is a very big business in dognapping. An ounce of prevention will keep a pup and a kid happy.

2 . . . Tar's surprised by the rough treatment . . .

3 . . . He's immediately yanked out of the car . . .

119

4 . . . He's given a good sound spanking, then . . .

5 . . . sent home. No more strange cars for him!

Slam the gate on him. He'll learn to be a gentleman, even if he does weigh more than she.

THE GATE CRASHER

Gate crashers, whether they be dogs or people, are bores and should be stopped. It's rather simple to correct the dog crasher. Close the gate on his neck as he goes through.

You may need an assistant to help in the correction. It will depend on how your gate or door is situated. When Towser bounds through the gate or door ahead of you he's just expressing his excitement. He likes to go out just as you do, but that's no reason for him to try to smear you all over the gate-post. First try to correct him with the yanking on the leash and the HEEL command. In his excitement this may not "reach" him. After trying this normal correction a few times with no success give him something to remember. As he passes through the gate ahead of you either you or the assistant close the door on his neck. Let him get his head caught. Use your head at the same time — don't let him get hurt. The bang on the head or a little struggle on his part won't hurt him. He'll remember this. The next time through, caution him with command HEEL. He won't be quite as anxious "to get over the mountain to see what he could see."

The stairs charger is another problem. Dogs will charge in both directions, up and down. If he charges up while on a leash, the correction is obvious — change your direction, go down. As he gets to the end of the leash, he'll change his direction with the added yank from you. He'll learn this one, head over heels.

Off the leash the problem is a little harder to correct. What usually happens is that you start to go up or down a flight of stairs, the dog comes from behind and wants to make a race out of it. Especially in a household where the kids run up the steps, the dog sees them walk across the floor, then take the steps two at a time. This quickening pace is what teaches a dog to bolt. Whatever the cause, he must learn that the race isn't a fair one — he has four legs, you only have two. Going down is easier to correct. Start down. When you hear him come on from behind, stop. As he passes you flip him off balance with your foot. A few such rolls will cure him. This may sound cruel. Remember, it's better for him to roll than for you — he doesn't fall from as high.

Going up the steps will take some fancy dancing on your part. A narrow flight is necessary. As he comes from behind, stop. As he passes you, pin his head to the wall with your knee just as we did with the gatepost on the gate crasher.

If your dog develops the habit of wanting to lean on your legs while walking, teach him to use his own. Every time you take a step whack him with your foot or leg. To accomplish this you'll be waddling down the street for a while, but it'll be worth it, especially on a rainy day.

If he becomes a sniffer when he's supposed to be a walker, you can usually control this by yanking the leash. If he persists, scrape your foot between the spot he's smelling and his nose. If this still isn't enough or if he starts to do it off leash, have an assistant walk behind you with the cans on a string (see page 116). When he stops to sniff toss the cans at him, startle him.

Part III

Chapter 8

You Should Know

Let's straighten out some misconceptions you should know about dogs, give you some important information and the latest medical advancements that will keep your dog healthy.

SEX — THERE'S A DIFFERENCE?

Male vs. Female ... An age-old question. Which is best? There's a feeling among dog people that a female makes the best pet. She's less likely to roam. This may be so, but I disagree with those who insist that a female takes to her lessons better. This depends more on how the dog is brought up. Males are just as affectionate as females, in my book. In many ways a male is more dependent on his master than the female. It's quite true that females are less likely to fight. They're the smaller members of the breed and the general opinion is that they're easier to housebreak. It's not necessarily true that they're less rambunctious, but many dog people think they are. Many feel that the female will understand your moods better — just female intuition, I guess.

Facts about the Female ... The only time that the female attracts the males is when she's in season. A bitch's first heat occurs at approximately nine months of age, then in most cases she goes on a six-month cycle. The heat lasts about 21 days. She'll attract males during this time, but she'll only stand for a dog about five days in the middle of the heat. An old English poacher's trick on nightly hunting expeditions was to take along a bitch in season. This was to lure the caretaker's watchdog from his post. Because the male can be diverted from his job, some folks feel a female is a more reliable dog.

Spayed Females ... make excellent pets. Their personalities aren't changed, and they don't become fat and lazy unless you overfeed them, with the exception of the very small breeds.

False Pregnancy ... is common among nervous bitches. They go through all the symptoms of pregnancy about nine weeks after the normal heat. They show signs of abdominal and breast swelling and even milk. They may go so far as to prepare a nest. This condition can be corrected with hormone injections.

Sexually Frustrated ... dogs and people, the world is full of them. The female dog will only express her sex urge during her heat, but the male is sexually alert all year. Dogs reared as house pets from puppyhood form close attachments to people and may respond with sexual overtones. If the male develops the habit of mounting a person's leg, the habit should be broken; it can prove embarrassing. Give him a good cuff on the nose and command NO. Give such a dog plenty of opportunity to run and exercise off his excess energy.

SOUP'S ON

Foods for Dogs ... meat (protein), cereals (carbohydrates), vitamins, minerals, fats, and starches are necessary, although he can do without the latter. All dogs, whether miniature or monster, can have the same diet — the only difference is the amount.

Number of Meals ... a day depends on the age of the dog. A seven-week-old pup has three meals; at six months he's cut to two unless he discontinues one of the meals of his own choice. A year-old dog gets one meal a day.

When To Feed ... depends on what you want the dog to do. If he's to be a watchdog he should be alert at night, so feed him in the morning and let him sleep all day. If he's a pet feed him after you eat, save him the scraps.

Don't Feed Him ... poultry bones, fish bones, brittle steak bones, or chop bones. They all splinter and can rip him internally. Don't feed sweets and raw eggs. The raw-egg routine for good coats is not true. It takes more energy to digest the egg raw than he gets out of it. Pork is hard to digest and should not be given even if cooked very well. Hard cooking will kill trichinosis worms that will kill your dog if he gets them in raw pork. Cauliflower, cabbage, broccoli, and parsnips aren't good for dogs and I tried to convince my mother that they weren't good for small boys — to no avail.

Fats . . . One major cause of dogs scratching is a lack of fat in the food. A normal amount of fat would be about 10 per cent. A working or hunting dog should have about 20 per cent while doing strenuous activity. Manufacturers of dry cereals and chows who advertise that their foods are fat-free are deliberately causing a false impression. Actually they can't put enough fat in their foods and sell it. The required amount of fat would stain paper or cardboard containers and make it unattractive to the buyer. If you use the dry meals, add fat to the diet — corn oil or bacon fat.

Meat . . . It doesn't make any difference whether you feed your dog ground meat or chunks. If the meat is mixed with meal a fussy eater will learn to pick out the chunks and leave the meal. If you have this problem, use the meat ground. The most nutritious meat is liver, but scrap from all parts of the animal, especially organs, are very nutritious for the dog. In the wild a dog eats the whole animal, everything from the pelt to the contents of its stomach. In that way he gets carbohydrates, vitamins, minerals, along with his proteins. This is how a dog in the wild provides a balanced diet for himself. Beef or horsemeat doesn't have to be cooked. In fact, it's preferable that it's eaten raw. An all-meat diet isn't good for your dog; he must have a completely balanced diet.

TIDBITS . . . Very often young pups nip fingers when food is being offered to them. This is usually not the puppy's fault. The trainer isn't giving the food to him in the right manner. If you hold the food above the dog's mouth and make him reach up and grab it, he's naturally going to open his mouth and clamp down while he's reaching. Fingers will then automatically become part of the tidbit. Instead of holding the food above the dog's head, put the food below the dog's chin level with a fast motion of the hand. Now he can see the food and take it with head down.

Commercial Foods . . . The advantage of dry cereals is that they're cheap and not much trouble to prepare — just add a little water or bouillon. They give a completely balanced diet, but it's important that fats be added and that the dog be given some meat. Canned dog foods are more expensive — you're buying a certain amount of water. A dog will usually take to them fast because they have good flavor appeal. Even with canned foods, the diet should be supplemented with other foods. Some vets consider the dry cereals so good that they recommend no added supplements.

Supplements . . . may be important in your dog's diet. A growing puppy should have a teaspoonful of cod liver oil every day. That dose should be cut for very small breeds. Your veterinarian may suggest a mineral supplement or a combination of minerals and vitamins to be fed once a day in the dog's meal. Pervinol is excellent. The vet may suggest a concentrated calcium to be fed until Towser's a year old. Let your vet decide about supplements.

Change in Diet . . . will make life a little more convenient for you. Some dogs become accustomed to only one type of food. If that food becomes unavailable they become a feeding problem. Get the dog used to all foods.

Skipping Meals . . . should not worry the chef if the dog's spirit doesn't seem to be affected. The digestive system is really built for his eating one large

meal every couple of days as he did in the wild. For this reason, an adult dog does very well on one meal a day. He may seem hungry because of the tantalizing smells that go on all day around the kitchen, but you'll do your dog more harm than good by showing your love with tidbits every time he feels he wants them. The sluggish, lazy, fat dog is really no fun.

Vim, Vigor, and Vitamins . . . The vitamins that are of greatest importance to your dog are A, B-complex, and D. Vitamin E is excellent for the dog's coat, the source of it being a wheat-germ oil. Vitamin D will prevent your dog from getting rickets and its best source is cod liver oil. Keep your cod liver oil refrigerated at all times or it will turn rancid and lose its vitamin content. The easiest way to give the cod liver oil is mixed right in the food.

The Finicky Eater . . . is usually the overfed dog. The dog's food should be placed on the floor and he should be given twenty minutes to eat. If he hasn't consumed it in that time the food should be taken up. Let him get the idea it's either now or never. If you're traveling with your dog it may take him longer to get used to the idea of eating under strange circumstances. It's a good idea to let him wait and get settled down before food is offered to him. The work dogs and hunters should be given plenty of time to cool off and rest after they've done a hard day's work before they are fed their main meal.

Amount of Food . . . The quantity of food varies with each dog. Common sense and a little experimentation is going to be necessary to determine the quantity of food your dog must have. For example, Tar, who you've seen all through this book, weighed 50 pounds by the time he was five months old. His brother, Arkie, weighed 37 pounds at the same age and was eating one-third more than Tar. The metabolism of these two dogs is obviously different. Everything that Tar ate seemed to turn into flesh. At age five months he was so heavy that he had to be put on a reducing diet; he still gained weight. Tar was very perky and happy with half the quantity of food that Arkie was eating at this time. A dog will quickly learn not to overeat. Experiment to see how much he'll take. A puppy should have all he can clean up. Pups usually won't get too fat. They shouldn't be like butterballs. As the dog becomes an adult, cut rations if he gets too heavy. If he's always begging and has no excess fat, increase his chow.

The feeding chart, opposite, therefore, is an approximation for general guidance only and need not be followed exactly. Remember that all dogs, whatever their size, can be fed the same diet, the only difference being in the

FEEDING CHART
BY EDWARD GRANO, JR., D. V. M.

AGE No. Feedings Per Day	SIZE	Weight in lbs.	AMOUNT PER FEEDING DRY 1 cup = 8 oz. by volume	SOFT-MOIST* 1 burger = ½ pkg.	CANNED 1 can = 14½ oz.- 15½ oz.
Weaning to 3 Months: 3 Times Daily or Self-Feeding	Small Breeds	3–6	⅓–½ cup	⅕–⅓ pkg.	3½–5½ oz.
	Medium Breeds	6–12	½–¾ cup	⅓–½ pkg.	6¼–9½ oz.
	Large Breeds	12–20	¾–1⅓ cups	⅔–1 pkg.	10–14 oz.
	Very Large Breeds	15–25	1–1½ cups	¾–1 pkg.	11¾–16½ oz.
3–5 Months: 3 Times Daily or Self-Feeding	Very Small Breeds	3–10	½–1 cup	⅓–⅔ pkg.	4⅔–11 oz.
	Small Breeds	12–15	⅔–1⅓ cups	½–1 pkg.	7⅓–15⅓ oz.
	Medium Breeds	12–25	1⅛–2 cups	¾–1⅓ pkg.	13⅓–22 oz.
	Large Breeds	15–35	1½–2⅔ cups	1–1¾ pkg.	15⅔–29⅔ oz.
	Very Large Breeds	25–50	2–3⅓ cups	1⅓–2⅓ pkg.	22⅔–38 oz.
5–7 Months: 2 Times Daily or Self-Feeding	Very Small Breeds	4–12	¾–1⅔ cups	½–1 pkg.	8–18½ oz.
	Small Breeds	12–24	1⅔–2¾ cups	1¼–2¾ pkg.	20–31 oz.
	Medium Breeds	20–35	2½–4 cups	1¾–2¾ pkg.	29–44 oz.
	Large Breeds	35–50	4–5 cups	2¾–3½ pkg.	45–57 oz.
	Very Large Breeds	50–90	5–6 cups	3½–5⅓ pkg.	57–83 oz.
7–10 Months: 2 Times Daily or Self-Feeding	Very Small Breeds	5–15	1–2 cups	⅔–1½ pkg.	10½–23 oz.
	Small Breeds	12–25	2⅛–3⅓ cups	1½–2½ pkg.	23½–37 oz.
	Medium Breeds	25–45	3½–4½ cups	2½–3 pkg.	40–51 oz.
	Large Breeds	45–70	4⅔–6¼ cups	3⅓–4 pkg.	52–69 oz.
	Very Large Breeds	70–100	6¼–8½ cups	4–6 pkg.	70–94 oz.
Adult: 1 Time Daily or Self-Feeding	Very Small Breeds	6–12	1–2 cups	¾–1½ pkg.	12–23 oz.
	Small Breeds	12–25	2–3½ cups	1–2⅓ pkg.	23–37 oz.
	Medium Breeds	25–50	3½–6 cups	2–3½ pkg.	37–57 oz.
	Large Breeds	50–90	6½–9½ cups	3½–5⅓ pkg.	57–85 oz.
	Very Large Breeds	90–175	9½–13½ cups	5⅓–9½ pkg.	86–152 oz.

* One package Prime or Top Choice equals 6 oz. One Gaines-burger equals 3 oz. (½ package).

amount they get. You should watch and see how your dog does and adjust the quantities you feed him accordingly.

Don't Worry If . . . your dog gulps his food down with table manners that would make a child look polite. The habit's a holdover from ancient times when dogs ran in packs and if he didn't get his food down fast somebody else would. If your dog eats manure he's just trying to obtain the partly digested grain that it contains. It means he has a craving for carbohydrates. This can be corrected by making sure he has plenty of cereals in his diet.

Taking Food . . . You can teach your dog that taking food from strangers is taboo. You'll need the help of a friend. Walk the dog on a leash. Have your friend walk toward you. When the friend meets the dog have him offer a piece of meat. As the dog goes to take it you command NO, yank on his collar. The friend shouldn't let the dog take the meat; he should pull his hand back. At the same time give the dog a rap across the nose with the other hand. The trainer who attempts this should have experience with dogs. This training can produce problems. It can make the dog mean if it is overdone. You may be causing a problem of feeding when someone else will have to care for Towser, such as the babysitter or the kennel man.

NO, NO startled him into dropping the food. "Look, Buster, you get a Grade A burger home."

THE STREET IS NOT YOUR DINING ROOM

A pup won't know the difference between food on the street and the food in his dish — they both smell good. It's rather simple to teach him to stop scavenging while on a leash. If you're fast enough with the leash you can yank his head up before he's able to pick the food up. In the case in the pictures, Tar picked up the food while Gretchen was looking the other way. Quick sharp commands of NO, NO may startle him into dropping the food. If not, open his mouth and take the food out. Scold him harshly.

CHOOSING YOUR VET

Let's talk about your dog's veterinarian. Some people have the idea he's some sort of a horse doctor — well, he is. But he's rather highly skilled. After all, how many people do you know who can talk horse-ese — that is, fluently? Thousands try unsuccessfully at the track every week.

You think your family doctor's pretty good? Try him in this situation. Walk into his office. Don't say the usual good morning to the nurse. Walk past her into the doctor's private office. Jump up on the desk and take off your shirt. Tell the same things to your doctor that the dog tells the vet — nothing. Now it's his job to cure you. But cure you of what! You haven't said — remember? When the doctor starts to ask you: "How did you feel yesterday? What did you eat? How are you sleeping?" etc., etc., just lick his face, whine a little, and look into his deep brown eyes. When he starts to poke you — growl. When he looks in your ears — scratch. When he says, "Say ahhhh" — bite.

Under such conditions the A.M.A. might want to consider socialized medicine. So you see, the vet has to do twice the work of an M.D. He has to ask the questions and answer them by himself at half the fee.

Don't blame the vet who wants to run a beauty parlor instead of a hospital, but stay away from him. Good veterinary medicine is a tough racket. It's a lot easier to make money clipping poodles. In fact, it's a pretty good job. Many a hairdresser would like to have clients that couldn't talk back.

You're going to have to have confidence in your vet, just as your dog has confidence in you. Don't be taken in by a flashy office or, for that matter, a dingy one. How does the place smell? Is it immaculate? How does he handle the dog? Is he interested? Is he a warm guy? Does he communicate? Do you think he knows what he's doing? Don't answer that one — maybe you don't know what he should be doing. If you did you wouldn't be going

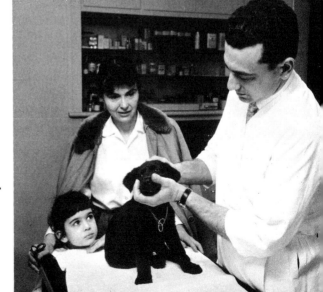

Tar's second-best friend is the veterinarian.

Etiquette in a vet's office is for everybody to mind their own business; that means dogs, too.

to him. Does he seem professional? Are his hands clean? What color is his white lab coat — gray? What color are his fees — green? Find out all you can about the vets in your area. Ask your neighbors, forget what they say, then make up your own mind.

Pick your vet and stick with him. Don't doctor-shop. Your dog's doctor will get to know you and your dog as he gathers some history from both of you. And most important, veterinary medicine isn't a one-way street. You're the one who's going to have to communicate to the vet for your dog. You'll have to recognize symptoms, observe unusual conditions, and accurately remember the order of things.

We'll be telling you some facts about the problems you'll face while acting as mother and, at times, nurse for your four-legged friend. We aren't in any way trying to make a veterinarian out of you, nor should you try to assume his responsibilities. We feel that if you know a little it won't be too dangerous if you use your information sensibly. Your only real job in this field is to help your vet solve the medical problems and then follow his instructions.

There's some basic etiquette that people should observe when going to a veterinarian's office. To put it simply and directly, I would say that people should mind their own business. The Good Samaritans who feel obliged to wander around the vet's office and pat and talk to every dog are more troublemakers than they suspect. Such a situation presented itself when Tar was taken to get his live virus inoculation at age nine weeks. A do-gooder type had brought her dog in for a clipping and a bath. Everyone in the office knew about it because she was explaining the problems of getting her dog bathed, as if it was a major problem of life. After she delivered her dog she went around to every animal in the waiting room, patting them, asking what was the matter, exuberantly spreading germs, expressing her love of animals, and saying good-by individually with some slushy talk. She finally got around to Tar, who was sitting in Gretchen's lap. As her hand approached the dog I said, "Better not touch, I think it's leprosy." That cured her.

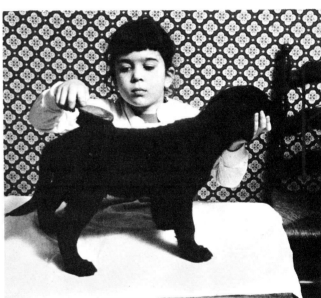

It was understood before the dog came home; his care was her job. She learns and he likes.

TAKING CARE OF OUR FRIENDS

When you made the decision to get the dog, you more or less made a contractual agreement between the dog and yourself as the trainer. The trainer would be the boss and the dog would blindly follow all your commands and be a devoted friend.

Combing and Brushing . . . lightly every day will prevent tangles and matting that cause dogs and children to hate getting their hair fixed. If a dog's coat is neglected it gets dull and it will be a terrible job to get him back in shape. Tangles have to be teased out with a comb. This isn't pleasant for the dog. You'll most likely have to resort to cutting the mats out completely. But before you resort to that, cut the mat into strands parallel to the hair. Take the fur close to the skin in your left hand and tease the matting out with the comb. If the scissors have to be used too much he's going to take on a rather ragged shabby look.

Long-haired vs. Short-haired ... has nothing to do with the intellectual ability of the dog you choose. It's going to take time and care to groom a long-haired dog. Long-haired dogs usually shed twice a year, but it can be practically all the time if a dog is kept indoors or fed a faulty diet. The short-haired breeds require no trimming or vigorous brushing to keep them looking their best. Needless to say, the short-haired or smooth-haired varieties are going to be less of a problem in keeping your dog looking fit, and the same will go for your house.

Burrs ... can be removed by rubbing mineral oil into the tangle. Work the burrs free with your fingers; this way you won't have to rip up his coat. Long-haired dogs that are going to work in brush cover should have the fur under their legs trimmed short so they won't pick up burrs. Burrs in the armpits will rub until blood is drawn.

Crew Cut ... not for your dog. His hair insulates him against summer heat and protects him from bites of all kinds of pesky insects. Close cuts will expose him to sunburn. Besides, short hair will prick and itch him.

Dandruff ... is just as undesirable in dogs as it is in people. It can be caused by parasites, too many baths with caustic soap, or a faulty diet. If you have it see your doctor; I'm not prescribing. But if Towser has it, seems free of parasites, and you don't suspect the bath problem, try increasing the amount of fat in his diet — a tablespoon of fat a day to keep the itch away.

Tails ... of the hunting breeds are often slashed at the tip from an invigorating run in heavy cover. Split tails take time to heal. Cut a finger from a leather glove, slip it over the sore tail tip, and fasten it with a round or two of adhesive tape.

Nails ... need some attention. A young pup's nails are like needles and the sooner you start regular care the better. He'll be easier to handle if he gets used to the idea at a young age. The guillotine-type nail clipper is the best. Have a friend help the first few times you trim his nails. It's only natural for the puppy to fight the restraint. Don't scold him — you'll only make the situation worse. Be firm; let him learn that nail clipping is something he's going to have to put up with.

City dogs usually wear their nails off on cement pavements; country dogs also wear their nails down by abrasion. It's the house pet that needs most attention. A good test as to when a dog really needs his nails clipped is to have him walk across a wood floor. If his nails click, they need clipping.

Hold his wrist firmly. Put the oval of the clipper over the nail so that the blade slides up from the bottom of the nail. It's best to clip a little at a time so that you don't cut into the quick. When you're finished, a few strokes with a file will prevent rough edges from catching things and splitting the nail.

The Collar ... for man and dog is unfortunately an uncomfortable necessity. Sooner or later both get accustomed to the ring on the neck, much as a bull gets accustomed to being led by the ring in the nose. Don't use a harness for your dog unless you're going to make him a member of a sled team. A neat flat collar with identification should be used for everyday wear and dress-up. As your dog grows, every once in a while test to see that he's not being slowly choked to death. Be sure you can always slip a few fingers between dog and collar.

The chain choke collar should be used for training. Be careful that this collar is removed before the dog is given his freedom to run. A choke collar that catches on underbrush can cause serious problems.

Dry Cleaning ... Towser shouldn't be confused with dry cleaning our woolen coats. Don't try to remove his spots with cleaning fluids that we use on our clothes or with bleach, gasoline, ammonia, and the like. If Towser comes home with tar or chewing gum in his coat, rub a piece of ice into the gum or tar. It'll become brittle and easier to remove. Dry cleaning is done with a commercial product bought at any pet shop. It's really a dusting powder. You dust it on, brush and rub it in, then you brush it out. A dog whose coat is kept clean won't have a doggy smell about him.

Wet Cleaning ... A dog should be bathed only when necessary. Weekly baths are entirely unnecessary. Too much bathing, except for retrievers and poodles, will remove the oil from the coat. Smooth-coated dogs only need a bath a few times a year. Lukewarm water should be used, make it about elbow deep. Put a rubber mat on the bottom of the tub so he won't slip and become frightened. Put a drop of mineral oil in his eyes to protect them from

Friend or foe...

WALKING THE PUPPY

One of the things puppy will learn to look forward to will be his daily walks. It should very definitely be the responsibility of the young trainer to see that puppy gets his necessary exercise, gets played with, and learns that this is the time to relieve himself. A three-month-old puppy should be taken out six times a day; a six-month-old should go outside four times; three times is enough for a year-old dog.

soap. Use a wet cloth on his face — dogs don't like water poured over their heads. Stuff cotton in his ears to keep the water out. Be sure to rinse him well, use a spray if you can. In the summer let him shake, in the winter dry him well. Rub him hard with a turkish towel. If you have a tank-type vacuum cleaner reverse it, use it as a blower. It'll dry him quickly.

Weighing... after the bath can be a real problem if you expect Towser to stand with four feet on the bathroom scale. Weigh yourself first. Then hold him in your arms and weigh both of you. The difference is him.

Scratching... isn't a way of life for a dog as many people think. A clean dog, free of parasites, won't scratch any more than you will. The worst time of year is the summer months. Your friend isn't going to stop until you do something about his non-paying guests — the parasites.

Parasites... such as fleas, lice, and ticks can cause a dog and the owner real misery. There are many species of each, but they all have one thing in common — they must have a warm-blooded animal to feed on. Fleas are the

most common; they should've been kept in the circus. All three can be carriers of such items as tapeworms, Rocky Mountain spotted fever, typhus, but the most common problem is the itching irritation they cause, first to the dog, and, if not controlled, to man. I've known families that have scratched so much they've had to move to the local motel while exterminators were called in.

Careful grooming is the first step in the control of all the external parasites. Look under the legs, in the ears, and between the pads on the feet. Ticks often get on the dog when he walks in the field. They don't move fast, so a check of the paws and between the pads after a run will catch many a tick before he can start causing trouble.

Tick control ordinarily isn't difficult. You'll be able to feel or see this critter. You can feel the lumps on a short-haired dog. But with any dog, examination consists of ruffling the hair against the grain so that you'll be able to see the skin.

To remove the tick, dip some cotton in alcohol and cover the ugly brute. This is to relax the jaws so that you can remove all of him. If you just pull him out his head may break off and the spot could get infected. Once you think he's had enough (and you can use drinkin' gin) slip a broad-headed tweezer on the top and bottom of him and gently pull. Disinfect the area.

The control of fleas and ticks is no joke, however, if your apartment becomes infested. Both, but especially the flea, like humans as well as dogs. There are a number of good anti-flea-and-tick products on the market for the dog and for your house. It's important to rid not only the dog of the parasites, but also his quarters and your home, or in a few weeks they'll reinfest the animal again and the cycle will start all over. Spray cans are the easiest to use; powders can be messy. There are quiet aerosol cans that will not frighten the dog. These sprays are very effective and are not greasy. One of the best known is Kemic. This product is made by Vet Kem Laboratories in Dallas, Texas. They also have a product to fumigate the home called Vet Fume. One female tick can lay as many as 2000 to 3000 eggs each time, and they can live two months without food. You can see that even if only 25 percent survive you'll have a real problem.

Mange . . . There are two types, Demodectic and Sarcoptic, commonly known as demodex and scabies. Both kinds are caused by mites and require professional attention. Positive identification is made by microscopic examination. Demodectic or follicular is caused by the mite burrowing inside the hair follicle, causing moth-eaten-looking patches which start on the head and face. This is the most difficult to cure. With Sarcoptic mange, the mite burrows into the skin, produces more intense itching and a thickening of the skin, which appears redder and more raised than in demodex. Scabies can be transferred to humans.

Ear Mites . . . live in the ear canal, produce itching and a brownish-black discharge. This can be passed to other dogs like other external parasites. It's best to get professional help for this since the ear is such a sensitive area. If it isn't too bad a case you can try to correct it by first cleaning the canal with mineral oil followed by peroxide on a cotton swab. Don't go too far down into the canal. Let the liquid float up the discharge. Dry the canal and apply 2-per-cent yellow oxide of mercury on a Q-tip. Give the ear three treatments five days apart.

Ringworm . . . isn't a worm at all; it's a fungus infection of the skin. It looks like its name — an oval raised lesion which starts small and gets progressively bigger. The hair becomes dry and brittle; so does the skin. To treat this, the dog must be clipped close in the affected and surrounding areas and all the clippings *must* be removed. The fungus attacks the hair itself and then infects the skin. Treatment with iodine or the many fungicides will destroy the fungus.

Eczema . . . a skin problem, is a confused issue which may or may not be caused by one of the parasites. It usually appears suddenly in the warm weather. Many vets feel it is caused by the flea. Angry-looking, wet, red and yellow patches appear. Check your dog's diet. In the summer cut the proteins. But make sure he's getting enough vitamin A and fat. If it's a persistent case, the vet should treat this one because it can easily be transmitted to humans. He'll treat it externally and internally with a fungicide. Treatment takes about three weeks. Too many baths can also cause eczema. I know some kids who would like their mothers to read that sentence.

Worms . . . are one of the major killers of puppies. There are more misconceptions about dog worms than any other problem in dog care. Some think that worms are caused by milk and can be cured with onions. Some think they can cure the problem with home remedies and commercial preparations bought at any drugstore. If you suspect that your dog has worms, a veterinarian should be consulted. Worm medicines are toxic and your dog might not only be suffering from worms — that may only be one of his problems.

Part of growing up is taking nasty medicine. Turn the page and see how Tar has to take his.

SOME HOME NURSING

1. A seriously hurt dog should be muzzled . . .

2 . . . gauze or string will do. Over, under, up and tie . . .

3 . . . Wrap it under his chin and tie it again . . .

4 . . . Tie off again behind his head; now he can't bite.

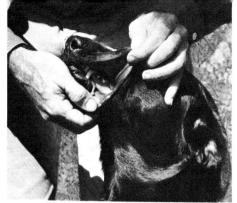

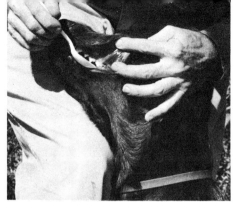

5. To give him liquids, form a cup with his jowls. Hold his head so that his nose is . . .

6 . . . tilted up. Pour the medicine off a spoon. It will drain into his mouth, he'll swallow.

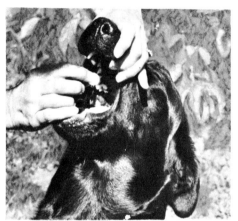

7. For pills. Squeeze his upper lips against his teeth. Force the jaws open. Drop the pill deep. Hold his jaws closed until he swallows.

8. For powders, they can be put in food as could be the case with other drugs but if a dog won't eat mix the powder in some butter . . .

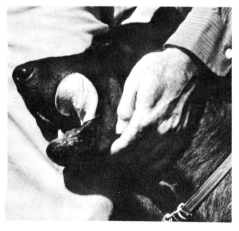

9 . . . Rub it along his teeth with your finger . . .

10 . . . With an uncontrollable reflex he'll lick.

There are five major worms that affect dogs: roundworm, tapeworm, whipworm, hookworm and heartworm. There are many outward signs that indicate the presence of worms. The dog may scratch; his coat will be dry and skin scaly. In some cases he'll lose his appetite and get in a poor condition while in other cases, such as tapeworm, he'll have a ravenous appetite. His eyes will appear dull and he'll act listless. Diarrhea usually accompanies the hookworm and whipworm. With tapeworm he mav drag his rear end on the ground, but this could also indicate that the anal glands need to be emptied.

Heartworm at one time was confined to the southern part of the United States, where the mosquito was so prevalent. Unfortunately it has now become a problem in all parts of North America. The mosquito passes an immature form of the worm from dog to dog. The adult worm lives in the heart and adjacent large blood vessels. It damages the heart, lungs, liver and kidneys and causes the dog to have difficulty in breathing, to cough, tire easily, become listless and lose weight. Although, when the disease reaches this stage, it can be cured, a lot of damage has already been done. If not treated in the advanced stages, heartworm will cause death. The only way to detect heartworm in the early stages is through a simple blood test. If found, it can be cured before it does any damage.

There is no vaccine to protect against heartworm but there are two methods of preventing infection. One is a daily medication that should be given all through the mosquito season and be continued for two months after the season has passed. It can be given all year round in warm climates. The other method is an injection twice a year to kill any worms that have started to develop. Heartworm is a serious business and your vet will know if it is prevalent in your area.

Some people feel that dogs should be wormed routinely. This is wrong. What should be done routinely, even if no symptoms are observed, is a microscopic examination of the stool. This should be done once a month until a dog is six months old, and twice yearly after that. It is more important to catch worms early than to wait for the symptoms to show. Worms lower a dog's resistance and make him easy prey for other illnesses.

Teeth ... aren't always as clean as a hound's tooth. Tartar will form a scale on the dog's teeth, force the gums to recede, and the teeth will become loose and possibly fall out. This, of course, can be corrected by removing the tartar. It's a job for the vet. You can help the situation by scrubbing Fido's teeth. This usually brings a raised eyebrow, but scrubbing his teeth isn't done with a brush; use a rough toweling. Wet it and dip it into table salt, which acts as an abrasive. Scrub the outside of his teeth with an up-and-down motion. This isn't a daily routine, but it should be done every few weeks. His breath will be better. Incidentally, while talking about teeth, it's not very sporting of a dog to bite a man. The dog has 42 teeth, while a man only has 32.

Teething . . . is just as difficult for a pup as it is for a child. There's no set time for the milk teeth to fall out, but the fourteenth week is usually the height of teething. It starts at age two months and continues until the pup is about six months old. The gums get sore and the whole system is upset. The pup may run a fever and have a little diarrhea. A good hard natural bone or one of the artificial ones will help ease the pain of his gums and help loosen his milk teeth; it will also help the tartar problem in adult dogs. He'll be less destructive around the house if you supply him with some good chewing material at this time.

Distemper . . . is the dreaded dog killer. It's a virus disease, and if your pup should get it the chances of survival are slim. The early symptoms are loss of appetite, diarrhea, nausea, a discharge of the eyes and nose, a dry cough, and a sensitivity to light. Sometimes the first sign is a spasmodic chewing as if the dog has something caught in his mouth.

Distemper spreads with terrible ease. The virus is transmitted through the urine, feces, nasal discharge, and saliva. It can even be transmitted through the air and carried by the owners of sick dogs.

There's no known cure for this disease. In only a matter of weeks it will drag a healthy dog down to the point where he will not be able to function. His nervous system is attacked, he'll have no motor coordination, he'll be blind and deaf, secondary diseases such as pneumonia will take their toll. The dog is really no longer a dog. If your pup should get distemper it's best to follow the vet's advice whether to try treatment or put the puppy to sleep. The author has tried to buck the inevitable and nurse a stricken pup who showed outstanding hunting ability. It was torment for the family and cruel to the dog.

But the distemper picture isn't all hopeless. Although there's no cure as yet, there's very fine preventive medicine.

It's very important when you get your dog that you get his complete medical history. Your vet will want to know what shots the pup has had and the dates.

Studies at Cornell University Virus Research Institute determined that live virus injections will protect a dog against the dread disease for a year. But it's important that certain conditions exist before the shots can be effective. Puppies, while in the kennel, are usually protected temporarily.

Almost every bitch passes on to her pups a natural immunity against diseases, including distemper. All pups in the litter get the same amount of protection, but the amount will differ from litter to litter from the same bitch. The problem is that unless the bitch is tested just before she whelps you will not know how long the immunity she passes on will last in the pups. Few bitches pass on no immunity; some pass on enough to last the pups until they are sixteen weeks old. The average is about eight or nine weeks. The length of time is the unknown factor. If the pup is given a protective shot while his mother's immunity is still in his system, the protective shot will not take. When your pup has had a shot before the mother's natural protection wears off, in spite of what you think, the dog will have no protection.

Here is the procedure to follow: for pups under nine weeks, in a clean environment with no contact with other dogs, no shots are given. If the dog comes from a kennel or a pet shop and his history is not known, you do not take the chance that the mother's immunity will protect him. For such a dog, under nine weeks old, a temporary live virus distemper or measle vaccine is given. If the mother's protection is in the system the shot won't take, but if it is an unprotected pup at this age, the vaccination will take effect. This puppy shot can be started at age six weeks and repeated again at the eighth week. At nine weeks of age all pups should get an adult dose of live virus vaccine. To guarantee that it took and that the mother's protection did not interfere with the immunization, the shot should be repeated four or five weeks later. Now, at the age of thirteen or fourteen weeks, 95 per-cent of all dogs will be protected. To be extra safe, and to make sure your pup does not fit into that 5 per-cent that are not protected, the dog should receive another shot between the sixteenth and seventeenth week. From then on the shot should be repeated once a year.

You can now see why it's important to keep the dog isolated when you bring him home at seven weeks of age. A nine-week-old pup, with his first protective shots, is safe to take into dog society. He should not be taken out until he has had at least his second puppy shot. Some people like to wait a little longer . . . it is a good idea to wait as long as convenient to make sure the immunization is well established in the pup's system. It's important in this procedure that the vet use live virus vaccine and not kill-tissue vaccine.

Hepatitis . . . is another virus killer. The symptoms are much the same as distemper, but in addition, the puppy's abdominal area is tender — he'll often hump himself up to relieve the pain. The mucous membranes of the mouth become fire red or yellowish indicating a general stomach poisoning. The disease spreads and strikes rapidly. There's a protective vaccine for hepatitis; it's usually given in combination with the distemper shot.

Leptospirosis . . . is a disease of the kidney. It's transmitted through contact with the droppings or urine of rats. Symptoms include: deep yellow color of the urine accompanied by an intensified urine smell, vomiting of a frothy white or yellow bile, muscular stiffness especially in the hindquarters. There is a vaccine available, but it's difficult to tell how long the protection lasts. If you live in a rat-infested area, a protective shot should be given every six months. Also, in such an area you should keep dry dog food in a metal container. Discard any sack or containers that rats have broken into — droppings or infected urine might be present. If your dog eats the food he'll get infected. It's possible for humans to contract the disease from an infected dog through cuts and abrasions of the skin.

Rabies . . . is a virus infection that can be transmitted only by a bite, the means of injecting infected saliva into the tissues of another animal. There are two forms of rabies, dumb and furious. Both forms have the same initial symptoms. There's a marked change in behavior — a friendly dog will get shy, or a shy one will become overfriendly. There's an avoidance of light and noise, a change in the voice, a refusal of favorite foods, and an inability to drink water. The throat becomes spastic, the dog can't swallow, and excess saliva foams and drools — thus the traditional picture of the mad dog.

In the dumb form the dog becomes mentally depressed. The lower jaw droops, he drools and makes no noise, he looks dumb. The throat becomes paralyzed, the jaw is "frozen" open, and the dog quietly awaits death, which will take place in a few days.

The furious form is just the opposite. The dog will roam and bite anything in his way. This is what accounts for the spreading of the disease. It is important that you never try to handle a dog that you suspect of having rabies. Which reminds me of the mean old man who, when bitten by a dog suspected of having rabies, requested the policeman who was applying first-aid to give him a piece of paper and a pencil. Asked why, he said, "I want to make a list of those I want to bite."

If a person receives a bite, no chances should be taken because if he's not treated immediately death is certain and in a horrible way — the victim dies in spasmodic convulsions. Any bite should be washed with a tincture of green soap and the name and address of the dog's owner should be gotten. Then medical attention should be obtained.

144

You, your dog, and people around you can be protected from this disease with a vaccination that should be given to the dog when he's about six months old. The vet will tell you how long the inoculation is good for — usually it's one or two years depending on the type of vaccine used. The tag he gives you should be attached to the dog's collar. A certificate of all inoculations should be carried with you on long trips.

This disease has been controlled to a great extent through public health education. In the almost 30 million dogs in this country, only .002 per cent had the disease last year.

First Aid . . . an injured animal may be frightened and confused. Even a normally gentle animal may bite or scratch the person attempting to help it. Therefore, the first thing to keep in mind is to protect yourself. If the animal injures you, you may then be unable to give it assistance. Injured animals often appear dead or in deep shock and unable to move. However, when disturbed, they will often use their remaining strength to run away. Therefore:

1. Approach the animal slowly and speak to it in a quiet voice.
2. Make a large noose from a leash, belt, string, or strip of cloth, and loop it snugly around the animal's neck.
3. If it appears that the animal may bite, have one person tie a string or bandage around its mouth while another holds the noose.
4. Control bleeding with a pressure bandage.
5. If the animal appears severely injured, cover it with a coat or blanket to keep it warm.
6. Call a veterinarian for further instructions.

To move an injured animal:

1. Lay a coat or blanket on the ground along and under the spine of the animal.
2. Gently roll the animal over on its back onto the blanket.
3. Hold the corners of the blanket and carry it as a stretcher.

Temperature . . . the universal indicator of health. It's not a difficult chore. Cover the bulb end of the rectal thermometer with a petroleum jelly. Raise the dog's tail and insert the thermometer about one-half its length. Hold it there for about a minute. The average normal temperature for a puppy is 102.5 degrees and 101.7 degrees for an adult dog. 103 in a puppy means little; 106 is high and means serious trouble. 103 degrees in an adult dog means trouble is starting and 104 means that you should call the vet.

Rest a dog before you take his temperature. Exercise will produce a higher reading.

For temporary control of a high fever until you can get to the vet, ordinary aspirin will do the trick. Give the dog one grain of aspirin for every seven pounds of weight every three hours. The standard five-grain tablet would be right for a 35-pound dog. Aspirins can be crushed and divided.

The hot dry nose routine indicating fever and meaning sick dog is just not so. A dog's nose is for smelling; the other end is for temperatures.

THIS IS THE LAW

Law . . . and your dog is mostly a local affair. There are so many laws pertaining to the dog in all sections of the country that it would take many volumes to present them all. Be sure you find out if your dog needs a license. Most areas require one. At what age is it required? Remember, paying for your dog's license doesn't give him the right to act like a dog. If you live in an apartment, does the fine print of your lease say no dogs? If you have signed it, your landlord can force you to get rid of the dog. Check to see if your community has a leash law. Some communities require a dog to be muzzled to roam free. Nuisance laws give your dog the freedom he wants until your neighbors complain that he's a pest; then you'll have to restrain Fido.

A game warden is within his legal right to shoot and kill a dog that chases deer. Certain states allow a farmer to put out poison to kill dogs that raid his livestock. Owners of dogs that have injured or killed livestock are liable for the damages.

Some states have compulsory rabies inoculation laws for the eradication of the disease. Practically all states have some provisions regarding rabies.

Bite cases are the most common in which suits for damage are brought. Common law states that a dog is entitled to one bite; after that the owner is responsible. If a person is bitten through his own negligence, the owner isn't liable. A person would be negligent if he trespassed, ignored "Beware of Dog" signs, or was teasing the dog. Dog fights can bring lawsuits. Local laws will determine responsibility.

If you plan to ship your dog by common carrier across state boundaries inquire beforehand about regulations regarding crating, inoculations, health certificates, and costs. Rates for transporting dogs across state lines are set by Federal law.

There are very extensive laws protecting animals from cruelty. Some states make cruelty to animals a criminal penalty and go so far as to consider cropped ears and docked tails forms of cruelty. Which reminds me, in such states you'd have to sell your dog wholesale, you couldn't re-tail him. You should be able to find out the regulations of your community through the local SPCA, your vet, or the local police.

A dog who barks incessantly, especially at night, is legally regarded as a nuisance. In an apartment it's sufficient grounds for your landlord to bring suit against you, break your lease, and dispossess you.

Our laws get all mixed up from time to time. Under the law you're not to harbor a dog that doesn't belong to you. So, if you feed the straggly mutt who shows up at your door, you could find your kindness leading to a police summons. The reason for this law was to prevent professional dognappers from picking up dogs under the guise of having found them. On the other side of the law, the statute books state that if you happen to take in a dog for any duration of time, whether he belongs to you or not, you're required to give him food and shelter as long as he stays with you.

To play it safe, you can take out insurance to protect you and the dog while you're at home or away. You can get a liability clause to cover the damage Towser might accomplish in hotels or coverage for his hospitalization if he's on the receiving end.

In Mississippi it's hard to know whether to take out the insurance on your dog or your chickens. The law states that a farmer can shoot a dog that is molesting chickens unless the chickens are bigger than the dog.

FOILING DOGNAPPERS

Identifying tags are necessary so that people can identify you as the owner of the dog, not so much for the identification of the dog. Your name, address, and telephone number will do the job. Never put Towser's name on the tag — that's the first thing a dognapper will look for. Have a good photograph of your dog at home, so that you be able to identify him if someone claims that he's their dog. Many owners are having their dogs tattooed either on the lip or inside the ear. Your vet can do this and it won't hurt the dog. It's positive identification.

The National Dog Registry is the best insurance you can buy to protect your dog from dognapping. For a fee of $15 you register your name and address and your Social Security number as your identification. This number is then tattooed on the dog's inner right hind leg. The fee covers all dogs you will ever own in your lifetime. There is no added charge for more than one dog. Tattooing is painless, takes only a few minutes and is permanent. The registry does not do the tattooing; it's done by your vet or through the auspices of kennel clubs or the Humane Society. Most of the medical schools

147

and medical laboratories in the country are cooperating with the registry and will not buy dogs that are tattooed to use in their experimental work. You can get an application by writing to the National Dog Registry, 227 Stebbins Road, Carmel, New York 10512.

THAT'S IT

Today is the eighth of the month. Both Gretchen and Tar have a birthday. Gretchen is seven years old and Tar is nine months. But both are quite grown up. It's a warm feeling for a parent to see what they've done for each other. Tar's schooling for living in our society is just about over; Gretchen has a long way to go. Gretchen says she's going to be a nurse, a dancer, a policewoman, or something. Tar yearns to go to school with her every day. But Tar has another job; he's well on his way to becoming a great partner in our duck hunting.

It's hard to believe that at only nine months a dog knows so much, behaves so well, and is such a pleasure around the house. He'll never need a psychiatrist — he's too happy, he enjoys himself.

It's also hard to believe that a child so young as Gretchen can handle the teaching situation so well. Being teacher gives her the opportunity to be boss. This is good for children since they are on the receiving end so much at this age.

Gretchen just came in and took my pencil, and now Tar, who retrieves everything, lifted a box of paper clips off my desk. . . . "Hey, you two, come back here!"

A job well done deserves a shake. Good show.

148

149